Secrets of
GOOD PARENTING

Secrets of
GOOD PARENTING

Dr. Brij Bhushan Goel
D.Ph., NDDY, PGDHHC, Ph.D.

STERLING PAPERBACKS
An imprint of
Sterling Publishers (P) Ltd.
Regd. Office: A1/256 Safdarjung Enclave,
New Delhi-110029. CIN: U22110DL1964PTC211907
Tel: 26387070, 26386209
E-mail: mail@sterlingpublishers.in
www.sterlingpublishers.in

Secrets of Good Parenting
Copyright © 2013 by Brij Bhushan Goel
ISBN 978 81 207 7994 5
First Edition 2011
Second Revised Edition 2013
Reprint 2018

All rights are reserved.
No part of this publication may be reproduced, stored in a retrieval system or transmitted, in any form or by any means, mechanical, photocopying, recording or otherwise, without prior written permission of the original publisher.

Printed and Published in India by

Sterling Publishers Pvt. Ltd.,
Plot No. 13, Ecotech-III, Greater Noida - 201306, U. P. India

> **Before desiring
> the child to
> understand us,
> we should try
> to understand the
> child.**

Contents

Preface	xi
Motherhood: a big achievement	1
The dream of every couple – desirous child	3
Before pregnancy	5
Boy or Girl	7
Pregnancy test	10
Embryonic and fetal growth	12
Care during the pregnancy period	15
Post delivery care	30
Mother's milk	33
Registration of birth	40
Immunization	41
Care of infant	45
Massage of the baby	48
Sleep of the baby	50
Crying (weeping) of the child	52
Parents' mutual affection – the best gift for baby	53
If both parents are working	55
When a house maid is needed	56
Sexual relations of parents v/s child	58
Family planning	59
Diet of children	61
Malnutrition in children	65
Thumb sucking by children	68
Teething	70

Activities of the infant	72
Children's temperament	77
Children's nature	78
Safety measures to adopt around children	81
Helpful toys in the development of children	83
Importance of playing	87
If the child is lethargic	88
Physical growth of children	90
Indications of disease through infant's signals	96
Natural treatments for common diseases in children	99
The problem of increasing obesity in children	107
Care of the eyes	108
Enhancing resistance power (immunity)	111
Problems of children	112
Autism	115
When the child is shy (diffident)	117
When the child is stubborn (obstinate)	119
When the child is hyperactive	121
Recognizing mental tension in children	123
Children will learn as they see	128
Make the children cheerful	130
Beating affects the child adversely	131
Maintain the self respect of children	133
Prevent deviation	135
Why do children run away (abscond) from home?	136
Befriend your children	137
Don't hover around the child all the time	139
Teach your child the right values	140
If the child steals things	142
Teaching children the value of money	144

Contents

Teaching children how to accept defeat gracefully	145
Discouraging superstitions (blind faith) in children	146
Discipline	147
Encourage the child	149
Formation of character	150
Enhance self confidence in children	152
Build a strong base of ethics in children	154
Emotional development of children	156
Social and spiritual development of the children	158
Realisation of responsibility	160
Enhance creative thinking in children	162
Your children and their friends	163
When children start asking awkward questions	165
Sexual education	167
Making young girls into ideal women	168
A child's insistence on not going to school	169
Sending the child to school is not the end of your duties	171
Create on ideal atmosphere for the child while studying	173
Letter of a father to the son's teacher	174
Tuition for the children	176
During the examination time of children	177
Parents ambition (dream) – burden on the child	178
When the child fails in examinations	179
Recognize the child's talent	180
Higher studies with the help of education loans	182
Financial planning	185
Sexual abuse	188
Avoid misuse of amenities	190

Sleeping disorder in children	191
Effects of television	192
Craze for mobile phones and internet	194
Save your child from cyber pornography	195
Teenagers and harmful addictions	197
Prevent criminal tendencies in the child	203
Adolescence/Teenage years	209
Generation gap	212
Abnormal children and their special care	214
Childlessness	220
Divorce and the children	222
Company of grandparents gives satisfaction to children	223
Children's job/occupation	224
Marriage of children	225
Daughter-in-law of a family	228
Inducing letter	229
Don't forget the old parents	230

Preface

If the parents give birth to the children then it also becomes their moral responsibility to nourish them, to provide them education, perhaps arrange for their marriage and make them able physically and mentally, so that they become self dependent in future.

It is important work for every parent to nourish their children, but they may be lacking experience. The main aim of this book is to provide information about the requirements and duties of the parents in the development of children.

If a child becomes lazy, selfish, a glutton and naughty due to excessive love and spoiling, then it is the fault of the parent(s) for being over indulgent. It is important to encourage or chastise a child at the right time and right occasion so that there is proper, all-round development.

We should always keep it in our mind that an infant always observes our behaviour and nature keenly and imitates us. He learns a lot from it. Whatever he is taught in his growing years is the base for his nature as well as his future behaviour. It is the essential duty for those who know these facts that they should control their bad habits and create a gentle and disciplined atmosphere in the house. For this, they should sacrifice whatever they need to in order for the child to acquire good traits.

Parents should avoid quarrelling and keep their sexual activities behind closed doors so that the children are not exposed to such an atmosphere too early.

The education of a child depends not merely on lectures but on examples set by elders. Their undeveloped mind is not able to understand the lengthy advices and strict instructions. They are perfect in understanding and adopting what is happening around them. So whatever they are taught, practical examples should follow. In this day and age, the ancient Gurukul tradition does not exist. In these days, there is no such atmosphere around school, colleges, colonies and neighbourhoods for such development of character. A child gets might learn more bad traits from his surroundings than good traits. In this state of affairs, it becomes even more important that the atmosphere at home is peaceful, respectful and moderate so that the children get inspiration for adopting good qualities.

If we are not of good character, do not pay respect to our elders, are ill-disciplined, do not help our family members, do not help the despondent and handicapped, do not show respect towards women, how we can we expect all these from our offspring?

Every parent wants their children to be good natured, but that depends entirely on how they are monitored. Bring up your child with full responsibility and interest so that they get positive development.

Like a craftsman or a potter, who can mould the stone and mud in any shape he desires, similarly parents can mould their children.

For many great historical personalities, much credit goes to their mothers for making them so eminent.

It is common to see that the children of those parents who have imbalanced personalities or bad nature also become somewhat like them. Routine work and behaviour has a great impact on the tender mind of children. Parents can, not only enjoy their own life by adopting spiritual thoughts and a balanced life style but this can also affect the children as well. Then they will all be mould in that system without any overt training.

No child is incapable of understanding the education given to them. When wild animals or birds can be domesticated, then there is no reason why the god's finest creation i.e. a human child cannot be given training in the desired direction.

The only thing we need to do is to give them appropriate guidance and motivation to follow the right way.

In many families, the father is emotionally distant from his children even though physically he is very near. Such a kind of father hurts the tender heart of children by their strict and aloof behaviour.

For the emotional growth of a child, it is very important that he should feel emotionally secure in his mind. Hence parents should know how to show emotions.

If a child gets complete love and affection during his childhood, then in future he will share it with his companions. But if he himself is deprived of love then, it will be impossible for him to share it with others.

Generally, many parents are busy trying to improve their economic conditions and over compensate children with material goods while ignoring their character building.

Growing up like that, children become very materialistic and often due to negligence by parents, fall into bad company easily. So children must be taught good traditional values from the beginning.

Our children are the precious priorities of our life. Our main responsibility is to provide them with good nourishment and atmosphere. To develop their personality is a miraculous and creative work. For this, careful vigilance is needed for a long period of time.

Children of any country are the future of that country. The progress, success and development of the country depend on the children of that country. Today's children are tomorrow's future. So it becomes necessary to pay much attention to the health, behaviour and traditions of children. The mother often plays the main role in it because the home is the first school for a child and the mother is the first teacher. The mother takes care of her children's health or behaviour. So the mother has a big responsibility in society.

Dr. Brij Bhushan Goel

Motherhood: a big achievement

To be a mother is a very emotional feeling for women, which she can perhaps not be able to express in words.

This gift which women have got from nature is a precious gift. Motherhood fills women with a sense of completion and surprise. The happiness that a woman gets from the birth of her child is perhaps incomparable. With the birth of a child, the life of a woman completely changes.

Everything fades in comparison to motherhood. A woman realizes that the happiness she gets by looking at the smiling face of her child may not be achievable by any other physical means. She loses herself in her child's different activities without any tension.

Most women, whether literate or illiterate, rich or poor, a career woman or a house wife, etc., do not want to be deprived of being a mother.

In today's' times, there is no doubt that being a mother is not such an important thing like it used to be. But a lot of career-oriented women, after they achieve their goals, often start feeling a sense of loneliness in their life without a child.

Motherhood is an important event as well as the greatest responsibility in the life of a woman. It is that passage of love and affection which every woman wants to pass. A woman starts feeling differently about everything. Her child becomes her first priority and other things become less important.

The happiness she gets from fulfilling the responsibility of motherhood is different from all the other successes she gets in her life.

There are certain women who become mothers but do know how to take care of the child. On the other hand, there are those career-oriented women who do not like the idea of motherhood. To be a mother is often the result of an accident for them. Taking care of the child becomes like a burden for them. However, if they want to, they can make their child an able citizen of the country. They are perfectly capable of doing that. The need is to understand their responsibility and try to take interest in it.

It is a desire of almost every woman to be a mother. But it is necessary to be a mother at right time. Some women put off having children till late due to their busy careers, which can have adverse affects on health. The reproductive capacity of a woman is approximately 13 to 45 years. To ensure the good health of both mother and child, the first 7 years and the last 10 years of the reproductive period are not very suitable. The best period for reproduction is between 20 to 30 years

The dream of every couple – desirous child

There is no creature in this universe that does not dream of having a beautiful, healthy and brilliant child. But in reality, only few parents are able to get such a child.

For this great task, parents should be mentally, physically and spiritually healthy.

To enhance the capacity of the reproductive power, it is necessary that before conceiving, men and women should not misuse their bodies and keep the body disease-free and healthy.

A woman is considered to be like the earth, as she has the same patience and nourishing power as the earth has. Thus the product of the seed depends entirely on what type of seed it is.

During conception, the child that is conceived will have the characteristics of the sperm that fertilizes the egg. So the parents should be of good character and should live a virtuous life. A virtuous mode of living cleans the internal system and results in strength, valour, good health and a strong mind and gives birth to a child of strong character.

So start including fresh vegetables, fruits and milk in your diet three months prior to the desired time of conceiving. Avoid eating late at night. Abstain from excessively spicy, sour, fried, non-vegetarian and stale food.

Do regular exercise and pranayama.

Speak pleasantly; get rid of the feelings of anger, greed and hostility.

The main priority of parents is to understand their responsibilities before the birth of a child and be prepared for them socially, economically, physically and mentally. From the birth of a child till his adolescence, parents need to be extra vigilant.

Before pregnancy

For a beautiful, healthy and brilliant child one should consider the following:

Contraceptive pills: Usually women use contraceptive pills nowadays. Don't use any kind of contraceptive pills before two months of conceiving so that all functioning of the body becomes natural. Stop other means of contraceptive and let the body work naturally.

Weight: Keep a check on your body weight during conception. If you are under weight, add nutritious food to your diet. If you are overweight or on the verge of it, avoid fat and starch in your diet.

Excess of weight is a hindrance in conceiving and creates problems during pregnancy. It also increases the possibility of a Cesarian baby.

Being under weight is also a problem for conceiving. Even if conception takes place, the health of the child will be affected.

Drugs: If you have the habit of chewing tobacco, smoking and drinking any form of alcohol, leave it immediately. It increases the possibility of the child being under weight and premature birth of the child.

Health check-up: It is important that both husband and wife should get a full health check-up done. For women it is necessary that they get fully medically checked before conception. If there is an irregularity, it can be cured before getting pregnant. It might become fatal if it is found during pregnancy. Many a times the body becomes anaemic or hormonally imbalanced which may cause abortion or miscarriage.

Adopt a healthy routine: Eat healthy meals which include fresh fruits and green vegetables. Have fresh sour fruits like oranges, lemons, amla (gooseberry), loquats and grapes. Their high content of vitamin-C helps in the absorption of the iron found in green vegetables. It reduces the possibility of anaemia.

The diet must be balanced, and gas forming or acid forming diets should be avoided. Adopt the habit of walking in a green and open environment and do Pranayama and other Yogasana which are helpful in strengthening the uterus, lungs and heart. It is important as they have to work more during pregnancy and delivery.

Suffering from any other disease: If you have a hereditary disease or a chronic disease, get it checked and get proper treatment. Don't get pregnant before the end of the treatment. Pay special attention to it.

If you are diabetic or have epilepsy, then strictly adhere to taking the dose of medicine fixed by your doctor.

Be polite and gentle in behaviour: If the parents want a child of a happy, smiling and charming nature, good character and behaviour, then it is very important that the behaviour of both husband and wife with one another and with others be excellent. Daily behaviour should be polite, gentle, intimate, helpful and self confident. Whatever qualities you want in your child, you should inculcate that in your character first.

> **During conception, whatever ideas come to the parents' minds as well as the picture they have in their heart and subconscious, the child will be born with similar impressions.**

Boy or Girl

1. If the man is breathing through the right nostril and the woman through the left nostril during conception, then it increases the chances of giving birth to a male child.

   If the man is breathing through the left nostril and the woman through right nostril during conception then it increases the chances of giving birth to a female child.

   Ways of changing breathing:
   - (i) Close the nostril which is active that time by pressing it, the breathing from the other nostril will start.
   - (ii) Lie on that side of which the nostril is active, this changes the breathing to other side.
   - (iii) Put a cotton ball in the active nostril and breathing will happen through the other nostril.

2. Modern biology believes that in the human reproductive cells (sperm and ova), there are 46 chromosomes in pairs of twos. Out of these, 1 pair is the sex determining (X or Y) chromosome. During conception, sperm chromosome combines with ova (egg) chromosome. The sex of the foetus is determined by these chromosomes.

   An egg has only X chromosomes. Sperm has X or Y chromosomes. A foetus with both X chromosome is a girl. And with one X and one Y is a male child.

   The sex of the foetus is determined at the time of conception.

So in the desire of a male child, pregnant woman should not be given those medicines which claim to give birth to a male child. It has adverse effects on the health of the child.

Note: In the desire of a male child, do not miscarry or abort a female child. In will have adverse effects on the health of mother in the future.

> **A son or daughter is not so important. What is important is a healthy and talented child.**

Expected Date of Delivery on the Basis of Last Menstrual Period

Jan.	1	2	3	4	5	6	7	8	9	10	11	12	13	14	15	16	17	18	19	20	21	22	23	24	25	26	27	28	29	30	31	
Oct.	8	9	10	11	12	13	14	15	16	17	18	19	20	21	22	23	24	25	26	27	28	29	30	31	1	2	3	4	5	6	7	Nov.
Feb.		1	2	3	4	5	6	7	8	9	10	11	12	13	14	15	16	17	18	19	20	21	22	23	24	25	26	27	28			
Nov.	8	9	10	11	12	13	14	15	16	17	18	19	20	21	22	23	24	25	26	27	28	29	30	1	2	3	4	5				Dec.
Mar.	1	2	3	4	5	6	7	8	9	10	11	12	13	14	15	16	17	18	19	20	21	22	23	24	25	26	27	28	29	30	31	
Dec.	6	7	8	9	10	11	12	13	14	15	16	17	18	19	20	21	22	23	24	25	26	27	28	29	30	31	1	2	3	4	5	Jan.
April	1	2	3	4	5	6	7	8	9	10	11	12	13	14	15	16	17	18	19	20	21	22	23	24	25	26	27	28	29	30		
Jan.	6	7	8	9	10	11	12	13	14	15	16	17	18	19	20	21	22	23	24	25	26	27	28	29	30	31	1	2	3	4		Feb.
May	1	2	3	4	5	6	7	8	9	10	11	12	13	14	15	16	17	18	19	20	21	22	23	24	25	26	27	28	29	30	31	
Feb.	5	6	7	8	9	10	11	12	13	14	15	16	17	18	19	20	21	22	23	24	25	26	27	28	1	2	3	4	5	6	7	Mar.
June	1	2	3	4	5	6	7	8	9	10	11	12	13	14	15	16	17	18	19	20	21	22	23	24	25	26	27	28	29	30		
Mar.	8	9	10	11	12	13	14	15	16	17	18	19	20	21	22	23	24	25	26	27	28	29	30	31	1	2	3	4	5	6		April
July	1	2	3	4	5	6	7	8	9	10	11	12	13	14	15	16	17	18	19	20	21	22	23	24	25	26	27	28	29	30	31	
April	7	8	9	10	11	12	13	14	15	16	17	18	19	20	21	22	23	24	25	26	27	28	29	30	1	2	3	4	5	6	7	May
Aug.	1	2	3	4	5	6	7	8	9	10	11	12	13	14	15	16	17	18	19	20	21	22	23	24	25	26	27	28	29	30	31	
May	8	9	10	11	12	13	14	15	16	17	18	19	20	21	22	23	24	25	26	27	28	29	30	31	1	2	3	4	5	6	7	June
Sept.	1	2	3	4	5	6	7	8	9	10	11	12	13	14	15	16	17	18	19	20	21	22	23	24	25	26	27	28	29	30		
June	8	9	10	11	12	13	14	15	16	17	18	19	20	21	22	23	24	25	26	27	28	29	30	1	2	3	4	5	6	7		July
Oct.	1	2	3	4	5	6	7	8	9	10	11	12	13	14	15	16	17	18	19	20	21	22	23	24	25	26	27	28	29	30	31	
July	8	9	10	11	12	13	14	15	16	17	18	19	20	21	22	23	24	25	26	27	28	29	30	31	1	2	3	4	5	6	7	Aug.
Nov.	1	2	3	4	5	6	7	8	9	10	11	12	13	14	15	16	17	18	19	20	21	22	23	24	25	26	27	28	29	30		
Aug.	8	9	10	11	12	13	14	15	16	17	18	19	20	21	22	23	24	25	26	27	28	29	30	31	1	2	3	4	5	6		Sep.
Dec.	1	2	3	4	5	6	7	8	9	10	11	12	13	14	15	16	17	18	19	20	21	22	23	24	25	26	27	28	29	30	31	
Sept.	7	8	9	10	11	12	13	14	15	16	17	18	19	20	21	22	23	24	25	26	27	28	29	30	1	2	3	4	5	6	7	Oct.

☐ Date of last menstrual period   ■ Expected day of delivery

If there it is a leap year (February of 29 days) during pregnancy, then add one extra day to the day if delivery.

Pregnancy test

Commercially available pregnancy kits are a rapid, sensitive, and accurate way of pregnancy test.

Urine collected in clean containers at any time of the day may be used in the test but preferably the first urine of the morning especially for the initial months.

Take out the CARD from the pouch.

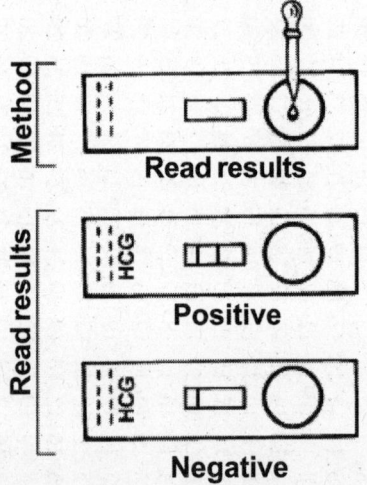

Dispense 3 drops only (approximately 0.1 ml) of specimen into the centre of the card by holding the dropper vertically, allowing each drop to soak before adding next drop. Wait for five minutes for coloured lines to appear. Depending on the concentration of hCG, positive results may be observed in as short a time as one minute. However, to confirm negative results, the complete reaction time of 5 to 10 minutes is required. IT IS VERY IMPORTANT TO USE 3 DROPS (or as recommended by the manufacturer).

Pregnancy test

1. **Positive** — As indicated in fig., the appearance of two purple coloured lines indicates a positive test result.

2. **Negative** — As indicated in fig., the appearance of one purple coloured line indicates a negative test result.

3. **Invalid** — When no lines appears at all, the test should be treated as invalid which may be because of improper storage at temperatures other than the recommended temperature, improper procedure or atmospheric exposure of the test device after opening the pouch.

Precautions

1. Use a new dropper for each sample, provided in each pouch.

2. Hold the dropper vertically when dispensing 3 drops of urine sample.

3. Do not open the pouch until you are ready to do the test.

4. Test units and samples must be equilibrated to room temperatures of 25-30°C before use.

Embryonic and fetal growth

End of the Month	Approximate		Growth
	Length	Weight	
1	0.6 cm	....	Back bone starts to form, heart forms and starts beating but not audible. Shape of body parts start forming, small buds forms which later grows in to hands and legs. Central nervous system appears.
2	3 cm	1 gm	Bone formation takes place. Arms and legs appear. Major blood vessels are formed. Internal organs continue to develop.
3	7.5 cm	30 gm	Eyes are formed. Nose and ears appear. Bone formation continues. Arms and legs are formed. Heart beat is audible. Urine formation starts. Foetus starts movement but mother cannot feel that. Body system continues to develop. Development of mind starts.

Embryonic and fetal growth

End of the Month	Approximate		Growth
	Length	Weight	
4	18 cm	100 gm	Head is larger compared to other parts of the body. Hair appears on the head. Many bones are formed. Limbs are fully formed. Skin is transparent. Joints formation takes place. Development of body parts fasten. All the seven elements form. Foetus desire & different things. This is why a woman is considered as having two hearts. Suppressing of desire put adverse affect on the foetus. So during that period the desire of a pregnant lady be fulfilled as possible.
5	25-30 cm	200-450 gm	Head grows less proportionate to rest of the body. Foetal movements commonly felt by mother. Rapid development of body systems. Mind is awaken.

End of the Month	Approximate		Growth
	Length	Weight	
6	27-35 cm	550-800 gm	Head slightly larger as compared to rest of the body. Substantial weight gain. Intellect awakens.
7	32-42 cm	1100-1350 gm	Head and body are in proportion. All parts of the body are clearly visible. A baby born in the 7th month may survive, but is very weak and needs special attention.
8	41-45 cm	2000-2300 gm	Subcutaneous fat deposited. Vitality remain & active. Vitality flows from mother to foetus and foetus to mother.
9	50 cm	3200-3400 gm	Foetus is completed with sense organ etc. In the 9th or 10th month delivery takes place.

Care during the pregnancy period

The pregnancy period is very important during which both mother and foetus require extra care. Thus maximum care should be provided, because the whole life of the child to be born depends on it. A little carelessness in this period could bring about a lot of trouble in the health of the child in the future.

During the period of foetal growth, in addition to the mother's, the co-operation of the husband and the whole family is also necessary. The period of nine months after which motherhood comes about is very important. During these nine months what she eats, what she thinks, what she does, what she reads, all these things determine the health and personality of the coming child.

A mother should follow that character during pregnancy and lactation periods which she wants to find in her to-be born child. The health and brilliancy of a newly born child depends on the food and life style of the mother. Many physical and mental changes take place during the pregnancy period. So during this time, it is necessary to follow a disciplined routine in various aspects.

1. Appropriate and nutritious diet

The base of health and development of a child is built during the pregnancy period. So the pregnant woman should take appropriate, nutritious and easily digestible diet so that the foetus may get proper physical and mental development.

Such as:
1. Milk and other milk products (especially sesame, soyabean, ground nut and coconut milk etc.)
2. Fresh vegetables — All leafy vegetables, bottle gourd, ridge gourd (tori), parwal, tinda, turnip, beet root, carrot, cucumber, spinach, tomato etc.
3. Cereals — Unpolished rice, flour with bran.
4. Natural sweet things — Honey, jaggery, dates, raisins and black raisins.
5. Sprouted cereals — Green gram dal, moath beans, wheat, alfalfa, groundnut and fenugreek seeds.
6. Dry fruits — Fig, cashew nut, almond, walnut (all in soaked condition).
7. Fresh fruits — All the ripened and juicy seasonal fruits like guava, pear, apple, banana, sapota (chikoo), sweet lemon (mausambi), orange etc.
8. Fruit and vegetables juices — Such as apple, carrot, sweet lemon (mausambi), orange juice etc.
9. Soup — Spinach, carrot, tomato, beetroot and coriander etc. prepared by mixing them or separately.
10. Other — Lemon-honey water, butter milk, coconut water etc.
11. Drink plenty of water.

It is better to take necessary minerals and vitamins from natural foods instead of synthetic sources (pills etc.)

Care during the pregnancy period

Nutritious element	Food items	Functions
Calcium	Milk and its product, wall nut, almond, pistachio nut, sesame, green leafy vegetables, ragi etc.	Necessary for the formation of bones and teeth of foetus.
Iron	Whole grains, dry fruits, green leafy vegetable (spinach etc.), fresh fruit etc.	Necessary for the formation of blood vessels in foetus.
Vitamins	Fresh fruits, green vegetables, sprouted cereals, salads etc.	In the development of different parts of the body.
Folic acid	Green leafy vegetable, fruits, cereals, seeds and nuts etc.	For the neuro system of the foetus.
Zinc	Cereals, nuts, oily seeds, fruits and vegetables etc.	For the development of tissues of the foetus.
Protein	Milk, dual seed grains, soyabean etc.	For the development of the body.

(Iron, calcium and protein should be taken in plenty in the diet).

Note – When fresh milk is not easily available, then dry fruits, sesame seeds (til) and sprouted pulses especially soyabean should be used. In the lack of fruits; green vegetables, carrot and other tuber-roots can be used.

Instead of costly dry fruits (almond, cashew nuts, raisins etc.), cheap dry fruits (groundnut, dates etc.) can be used.

Meat, fish and egg should be avoided as far as possible. It produces toxins in the body. In the countries where meat, fish and eggs are essential, they should consume fruits and green vegetables in excess so that the toxicity may be neutralised.

Generally it is seen that a pregnant woman desires to eat sour food. So she should eat lemon and amla. If she desires to eat clay, she should take calcium pills.

If the food is not as nutritious as desired, then she should take iron pills, calcium pills, folic acid mixture, vitamins pills or mixtures etc. as supplements on the advice of a doctor.

Generally pregnant women are given excess of food which results in many diseases. Don't eat more than necessary but don't remain hungry either.

Special—When a pregnant woman consumes 300 ml of orange juice daily during pregnancy, there are high chances of the child being good looking. If a woman eats coconut and drinks coconut water daily during pregnancy, then there is an increased possibility of her giving birth to a healthy and fair complexioned child.

70% of the meals during pregnancy should be uncooked food (fruits, vegetables, sprouted food, dry fruits, and nuts). It destroys the accumulated toxins in the body and the body remains healthy.

In uncooked foods, natural minerals and vitamins are in sufficient amounts which help in the development of the foetus. Hence a healthy beautiful and brilliant child is born with a sound immune system.

Last two to three weeks diet—generally, the above given diet is sufficient but in last two to three weeks before delivery, she should remain on a diet of curd, milk, oranges, lemon juice, amla, other seasonal fruits and raisins, black raisins, dates, figs, etc. It is even more beneficial.

Prohibited Food—A pregnant woman should not take the following foods:

1. Flour without bran, maida (refined wheat flour), and polished rice.
2. Unripe fruits or vegetables.
3. Too much cooked food.
4. White/refined sugar, preserved food.

Care during the pregnancy period

5. Fried or roasted and flavoured food.
6. Sweets and all type of synthetic food.
7. Junk food, stale food, spices.
8. Excess use of drinks having caffeine (tea, coffee, soft drinks etc.).
9. Wine and intoxicating products.
10. Toxic food like meat, fish and eggs etc.

2. Physical cleanliness

The accumulated waste of the body must be passed out every day. Physical cleanliness is always necessary. This becomes even more important during pregnancy, as during this period, the chances of infection in a pregnant woman increases and so body cleanliness is necessary specially of the sexual organs, nipples, eyes, nose, ear, mouth, teeth, skin, hair and nails.

3. Clothes

Wear the clothes according to season. For better blood circulation in the body, the clothes should be appropriate. Cotton and other natural fibre clothes are much comfortable. Don't tie your clothes tight on your waist.

During pregnancy, always wear loose clothes. Tight clothes increase the possibility of a handicapped child.

During the selection of a bra or bodice, give attention that your nipples are not pressed. Wear such clothing which gives support to the breasts, covers the tip of nipple but does not press them.

To keep the breasts in shape, wear appropriate supporting bras during pregnancy.

Don't wear high heel slippers or shoes as they can become the reason for miscarriage (if you trip or fall). High heeled shoes also can make a pregnant woman tired.

4. Work

A pregnant woman should work like a normal woman during pregnancy, but should be careful while doing some physical work. Don't stand on stool, tables of much height. Don't lift or draw heavy weights. Save yourself from falling down. Don't use stairs frequently.

If servants or attendants are available at home, then a pregnant woman should walk around in an open environment and do light exercise at home.

If the pregnant woman is working, then she should continue with her work but should avoid such work which makes her tired or requires her to sit or stand in one posture for long time. If such work is necessary, then take frequent rest in the middle of the work.

5. Rest

The body needs rest during pregnancy. So take a minimum rest of 8 hours at night and 2 hours in the day time. In the last three months or last six weeks of the pregnancy, take extra rest.

Don't lie on your back as it may cause backache. It may disturb the digestion, respiration and circulation in the body. When you lie on your back, then all the load of the uterus weighs heavily on all the main veins and arteries of your body.

Always sleep sidewise and bend your leg a little. This helps in the proper circulation of blood in the foetus.

Care during the pregnancy period

Don't sit for a long time and after sleeping, when you get up, be careful. Bend your legs and get up on the left side.

Don't sleep too much during the day time and don't stay awake for long periods at night.

6. Travelling

Avoid travelling. If travel is necessary, then travel by train rather than by air. Use the bus instead of auto rickshaws. Consult your doctor before going on a long journey.

7. Intercourse (Copulation)

Avoid sexual intercourse for the first three and the last three months. If there is no problem, than intercourse is possible but pay attention that the position during intercourse should be right and it should not put pressure on the abdomen.

8. Weight

If the weight and health of the woman is normal, then the child will be healthy. The other's haemoglobin count should not be less and BMI should not be less than 18.5. If the woman is weak, then the weight of the woman during the pregnancy should be raised by 20 kg. If the mother's weight is more than normal, then let it not rise during the pregnancy.

10 to 12 kg weight is usually gained during the whole pregnancy period. ½ kg per month during the first three months and ½ kg per fortnight in the next three months and ½ kg per week during the last three months of the pregnancy.

9. Thoughts and emotions

The foetus gets affected by the thoughts and emotions of the mother. So for best results, a mother needs to care of the following things during pregnancy:

1. Make your thoughts pure and keep your mind cool and calm. For this, reading of good books, joining pious gatherings, concentration on spiritual things can be done.

2. Keep your vision holy and pure. For this, always look at the positive side and surround yourself with good company.

3. Listen to pure, holy and virtuous speech.

4. During pregnancy, be positive and optimistic. Be spiritual and read the biography of great personalities. Be cheerful.

5. Don't criticise anyone and don't listen to the criticism of anyone.

6. Keep away from jealousy, hatred and retaliatory feelings.

7. Adopt positive, virtuous and creative thoughts.

10. Tension

The foetus gets badly affected by tension. Search out the causes of tension and try to remove them. You must not be obsessed with the sex of the child. Don't let the fear or doubt enter in your mind because these are your enemies.

Have a routine for doing chores. Prepare clothes, mat, cradle, and mosquito net and bed sheets for the coming child. Read books that are related to child care. If you are interested in religious books read them also. Use your spare time to read the childhood of great personalities, epics of heroes, cultures of different countries, history, books and magazines which give tips for a happy married life. Don't let any tension come in your mind. Be happy in difficult situations also. It will be foolishness, if you get excited needlessly. Anger, hatred, jealousy, enmity are considered weaknesses. Don't let them come anywhere near you during pregnancy.

Sit with your eyes closed. Imagine a beautiful view and think that you are holding the baby in your arms. Visualise the child and talk to him/her.

11. Yoga and naturopathy

By adopting naturopathy and yoga steps you can get the happiness of being the mother of a healthy child.

Yogasana advices for pregnancy and normal delivery —

1. Asana — vajrasana, sukhasana, tadasana, shavasana etc. and other easy asanas.

2. Pranayama — Do this in clean and fresh air deep breathing (inhale and exhale), Nadi shodhan.

3. Meditation — Sit in sukhasan. Concentrate and meditate for 10 minutes each every morning and evening.

4. Prohibited — Kapalbhati, uddiyanbandh, nauli, kunjal, surya namaskar and difficult asanas are prohibited during pregnancy.

   Avoid all such exercises which are painful and cause strains.

Naturopathy advices for pregnancy and normal delivery —

1. Morning walk for ½ hour.
2. Cold hip bath.

3. Mud pack on the abdomen.
4. Sunbath.
5. Light physical exercise, and other light exercises must be done and exercise deep breathing in open fresh air.

12. Non suppressible urges

Don't suppress the urges for defecation, urination, hunger, thirst, sleep etc.

13. Knowledge enhancement

The mind of the foetus starts developing from three months of pregnancy. By reading knowledgeable literature and by having knowledgeable talks during pregnancy, the foetus imbibes knowledge.

14. Sleeping room

Hang good pictures in your sleeping room. It gives positive effects to the coming child.

15. Smoking

The child of a woman who smokes may have mental disorder. Smoking increases psychiatric problems. So avoid second hand smoke too.

16. X-ray

Avoid X-ray and other types of radiation during pregnancy.

17. Important instruction

Even though the use of T.V., computer, microwave is not harmful, still, to save you from electromagnetic radiation, generally keep a distance of 2 feet away from electronic devices.

All the instructions related to mobile phones are applicable to pregnant women, so keep the phone away from the heart. Don't sleep with mobile phones close to you.

Environment — A pregnant woman should remain away from the pollution and pesticides.

18. The duty of a husband

The responsibility of a husband increases when the child is in the womb. Though the responsibility of housework often lies on a woman, but during the time of pregnancy, pay special attention to the diet, exercise, rest, happiness and good company of the pregnant woman. Co-operate with her in every work willingly. Whenever a husband finds that his pregnant wife is gloomy or tense then he should try to change her mood by talking lovingly and kindly.

19. Physical problems during pregnancy

Every woman goes through some physical problems during pregnancy. Some get cured by themselves and some others by adopting precautions of proper diet and life style or also by general treatment.

Vomiting — Vomiting and nausea are common problems during the starting period of pregnancy. This condition rises due to excess hormone secretion in the body of women.

Some remedies for nausea and vomiting include drinking pomegranate juice and coconut water. Also, cut lemons and put black pepper and salt and suck on them after warming them a bit to stop vomiting.

Abdominal pain—Abdominal pain may be due to many reasons. The pain is due to the growth of the foetus. Sitting or lying down in a comfortable position gives relief.

Constipation—Constipation is a common problem during pregnancy. Drink plenty of water; eat fresh fruits and fibrous vegetables. Use of these things prevent constipation.

Isabgol or one table spoonful of triphla can also be taken at night.

Swelling up of the hands and legs—Swelling starts due to the retention of water and physical changes in a woman during pregnancy. Lack of protein and high blood pressure are also the causes. Avoid oil and salt in your diet.

Back pain—Due to the growth of the foetus, the weight supported by the muscles increases, so back pain starts. Don't use any type of medicine for this pain. In case of continuous pain consult your doctor immediately. Avoid heavy weight and try not to bend during pregnancy.

Frequent urination—After conception, the woman feels the need to urinate frequently. It is not a disease or deformity. Due to enlargement of the uterus, the pressure increases on the bladder. It causes frequent need to urinate. If you think that the problem is increasing, consult your doctor.

Morning sickness—There is often a feeling of nausea in the mornings. Heaviness in the head or feeling giddy is also common. Have a fruit before leaving the bed and don't get out of bed immediately. Don't eat excessively at night. If you feel hungry at night, take fruits. These problems persist for first three to four months of pregnancy. But the secretion of hormones which causes morning sickness is good for the child and mother.

Care during the pregnancy period

Continuous fatigue — Feeling tiredness during pregnancy is a common thing, because extra energy is utilised for the formation of the foetus. Have minimum 8 hours sleep at night and 2 hours sleep during the day.

Itching — Many pregnant women complain of itching on the skin during pregnancy, generally around the stomach area and on the nipples. It happens in the 2nd and 3rd trimester. Actually the body is growing at this time and hence to accommodate it, the skin stretches and the itchy feeling happens.

White lines on the stomach — Regular massage on the stomach with mustard oil during pregnancy prevent these lines (stretch marks). Rub with a soft cloth at the place of itching. Don't scratch with nails.

Vaginal secretion — A little secretion during pregnancy is common. This can be easily cleaned. Pay attention to self cleanliness. If there is excessive secretion, then consult your doctor.

Burning sensations in the chest — Generally women complain of burning sensations in the chest during pregnancy. A pregnant woman should take light and easily digestible food in this situation. Avoid stale, sour, fried and spicy food.

Due to lack of calcium, stretching cramps starts on the legs. Increase the calcium content in your diet. Take calcium tablets regularly.

Fainting or swooning spells — If you feel faint, then lie down with your feet in a little upward direction. Take a right or left turn. Don't stand for a long time. Don't run here and there unnecessarily.

Gas and acidity — Avoid having fried or roasted and heavy food.

Spasms – Massage the affected organ, bend the legs and stretch.

Toxaemia – Happens when the blood pressure drastically increases during pregnancy. Sometimes it increases so much that it becomes fatal for both the mother and child. To avoid this, take less salt and eat uncooked food.

Note – Keep yourself healthy by eating a proper diet and maintaining a life style which will prevent you from needing any type of medicine. If it is necessary to take medicine, then consult your doctor first.

20. Daily checkup of a pregnant woman

Get the pregnant woman checked regularly so that any illness can be identified soon. During the first five months, a routine checkup should be done every month, after that twice a month and in the ninth month it should be done every week.

Apart from these regular ones, get checkups done also whenever necessary.

Get your blood pressure checked regularly. If it is 140/90 or more, then it is a dangerous sign.

21. Immunization of a pregnant woman

In the fourth and fifth month or the fifth and sixth month of pregnancy, a woman is given tetanus immunization

22. Necessary tests

The following tests should be performed – Haemoglobin, calcium, blood sugar, urine and HIV test. These are to be done every three months.

Care during the pregnancy period

If there is no problem, then ultra sound is done thrice, in the second month to know the heartbeats of the foetus, in the fourth month to see the development of the foetus and in the last month to plan the delivery of the child by seeing its position. If a physician feels it is necessary, then he can get it done at any other time also. And for further examination, a triple test can also be recommended.

Tests are also conducted for thyroid problems and thalassaemia. If both parents show symptoms of thalassaemia, then the chances for the child to have it also increases. If the child is found infected after testing, then it is better to get it aborted.

To see whether your blood group is Rh+ or Rh−, a blood test is conducted. If you are Rh− then your partner must also be tested. If both are negative then there is no cause for worry.

23. Painless delivery

For attaining motherhood bearing the delivery pain can be emotionally fulfilling. A woman bears this pain in the hope that she is going to be a mother. But today women show much fear at the very mention of the word 'delivery pain'. So they want the painless procedure which has become quite common nowadays. This procedure of painless delivery is called epidural anaesthesia. Use of it lessens pain during delivery. But it is better to avoid all types of medicine. Let the delivery be as natural as possible.

The woman who feels much pain during delivery should take the juice of basil leaves. It gives her relief from that pain.

Post delivery care

Go for urination immediately after delivery. This secretes out many unwanted liquids from your body. The first stool may be after two days. This is no cause for worry. Start feeding the baby. It will reduce the pain.

Start exercise and morning walks soon. This will bring your stomach and uterus back to the normal position.

Excess weight gain is seen after delivery by the lines seen on the stomach, thigh and on the nipples. You can get them cleared by reducing weight, by massages and by wearing a nursing bra.

Special Note – Keep the newly born baby on your stomach and love him. This process will stimulate the growth of the child. After the first few days, take the baby out for some fresh air for a short while.

For the new mother

1. After delivery the mother should not take cold water for 40 days.

2. Eating a small quantity of celery seeds (ajwayan) daily increases the appetite of the mother and helps food to be digested, gas to be passed, back pain reduced and uterus get cleaned.

3. The mother should drink hot vegetable soup many times in a day.

4. Give simple, light and easily digestible food to the new mother. Milk, dry fruits and honey is useful.

5. The mother should get massaged by a nurse or any other women. This brings the stretched skin back to its normal form.

6. A new mother should protect herself from cold wind, cold drinks and cold food. She should cover herself with warm sheets from head to leg.

Shrinking of the Uterus

After delivery the uterus is about 35 cm × 20 cm (approx. 950 gm in weight). After the mother starts breast feeding the baby, the uterus starts shrinking. Blood oozes out and the weight becomes half in a week. After six week it becomes 8 cm × 5 cm (approx. 55 gm in weight) and the size of a pear. This miraculous change does not occur in any other organ. For those mothers who avoid breast feeding, their uterus take longer time to come back to normal and they have to do many things to achieve that.

Some Yogasanas after delivery

After one month of normal delivery, for your health and to make your uterus and ovary normal, healthy and strong—

1. Bhujangasana, Uttanpadasana, Konasana, Tadasana, Urdhvahastottanasana and Shavasana etc. should be practised which can be performed easily.

2. Nadishodhan pranayama also but if necessary all the pranayama.

3. Meditation and Yognidra.

Restarting of menstrual period

After delivery, there is no fixed date for the restarting of the menstrual period. Some women take one year. But don't assume conception will not take place in this period. Egg formation will continue as usual every month. For some women, the menstrual period restarts after two or three months. But usually it takes 6 to 10 weeks.

Intercourse after delivery

Don't be hasty for sexual intercourse after delivery. Generally after two month of delivery, a woman is considered fit for intercourse.

Mother's milk

The mother's milk is best for the new born baby. No other food can replace it. It has the entire amount of nutritional elements which is needed by a new born baby for its growth.

It is important for the mother and the new born baby that breast feeding starts about half an hour after the delivery.

Both mother and child get a mental relief from breast feeding which is necessary for the development of a child.

In the initial two or three days after delivery, viscous milk comes out which is called colostrum.

It has many substances formed in mother's body which prevents many diseases. These elements protect the child from infections and diseases at that time.

Colostrum has such substances which protect the child from asthma and eczema.

It is also rich in protein, minerals and vitamins. It is that food which must be given to the new born baby.

Thus the new born baby should be given mother's milk from the beginning.

For the first six months, breast feeding is sufficient. Don't give any other external food. Even water is not required.

Start complementary food after six month for the development of the growing infant and you may continue breast feeding for two year or even after, if it is possible.

Advantages of breast feeding for the baby

The mother's milk is fresh, at the right temperature and available all the time.

It is easily digestible for the baby.

It has the best protein and minerals in the right proportion.

It is very nutritious and is formed in such a way that

all the nutritious requirements of a new born baby will be fulfilled. It has hundreds of such substances which are not found in cow's milk.

Breast fed children do not suffer from constipation and there is no smell in their stool.

The mother's milk is germ/bacteria free and so it reduces the possibility of diarrhoea.

It reduces the chances of skin diseases like eczema, red spots on the skin, and allergy of the new born baby.

The baby can drink milk according to his/her desire and requirement.

Such children do not face teeth problems in the future.

Mother's milk has many such substances which protect the child from many diseases in their initial growing stage.

Those who drink breast feed for a longer time have good physique.

It is seen that IQ and intelligence levels are higher in those who breast feed for a longer time.

Due to the physical attachment of the mother and baby, there is more love and intimacy between them, which is necessary for the mental development and health of the baby.

Advantages of breast feeding for the mother

Breast feeding by the mother to her baby is a natural phenomenon. Adopting it is beneficial to the mother as well as to the new born baby.

Due to this, menstrual period restarts late and this is beneficial for the mother.

Breast feeding is helpful as a natural contraceptive too.

It improves the process of osteoblast (the formation of bones) in the mother.

Breast feeding helps prevent diseases of the breast, including breast cancer, in the future.

Sucking of nipples by the baby helps the uterus to shrink back to normal size after delivery. It means the reversion of uterus to normal form is done in the right way.

The main advantage of breast feeding is that it enhances the feeling of motherhood and self confidence in the mother which results in an enhancement of emotional closeness between mother and child.

Diet of a breast feeding mother

From the birth of the child up to the feeding period, the mother should control her diet, life style and behaviour. Remember, all these things have a great effect on the baby.

Bleeding after delivery makes the woman weak and feeding reduces vitamins and minerals from the body of the mother. It is necessary to make them balanced with a nutritious diet.

The diet should be qualitative rather than quantitative. The mother's food should be rich in protein, calcium and iron. Vitamin B and D are highly required.

Just like during pregnancy, a mother should have a full nutritious diet even during the lactation period. It should include seasonal fruits, green vegetables, dates, presoaked dry fruits, nuts (almond, pistachio nut, cashew nut, walnut, raisins, groundnut, etc.) and drink milk in plenty.

The mother should take plenty of juices and water so that sufficient milk for the baby may be formed. Orange can play a big role in it.

Don't take sour, spicy, very hot or very cold food which may deteriorate the health of the baby.

Don't ingest tobacco, gutkha, betel nut or smoke and drink alcohol, etc. which affects the health of the baby badly.

A child gets a different taste from breast milk. Try not to take any kind of medication during breast feeding, as all the medicine may pass through breast milk to the baby and affect his/her health.

Use of hormonal contraceptive is a hindrance in the formation of milk. So don't use them while you are breast feeding. For contraception, use other modes such as condom, copper-T, etc.

How to Breast Feed?

Before feeding, if possible, sponge the breast, especially nipples with a wet cloth.

The mother should feed the baby sitting at a convenient place peacefully and with pleasure. While feeding, the head of baby should be kept in an upward direction in the lap of the mother.

Sit in sukhasana position peacefully and lay the baby in your lap, hold the nipple with one hand and put it in baby's mouth and rub the other hand affectionately on the head of the baby. This reassures the child and will build a good mental health in the future. During feeding, the mother should keep looking at the baby gently. Think of wellness and have good thoughts for the baby. Sing melodious and patriotic songs for the baby.

Don't feed baby while lying down as it increases the possibility of ear diseases in the baby.

Feed the baby in the right position so that swelling does not occur in the nipples. If the position is good, you can breast feed for a longer time without feeling uncomfortable.

While feeding, keep your attention fully on the baby. Think of his good physical and mental health at this time by keeping love, affection and mercy in your heart.

A baby takes about 10 minutes to get full, approximately. But all babies are not the same. So some may take more than 10 minutes other may take less than 10 minutes.

Feed your baby at least 8 to 12 times around the day. It will enhance the quantity of milk in mother and the baby will remain happy.

Don't feed baby when he does not require it. Don't think the baby is hungry every time he cries. Feed the baby from both the breasts. Feed him from the other if the first is emptied. This satisfies his hunger and he will get full nourishment. Let the baby drink milk fully from one breast and if he still wants, then offer the second, but don't force. Remember that you have to feed with filled breasts next time. Continue with this process.

Pay special attention to the nipples, as they get cut/ crack sometimes.

If a woman has had her first child or is weak or breast feeding is difficult, then wash the nipple with luke warm water before feeding milk. It makes them tender. After feeding, massage the nipple with butter or ghee. It makes them soft.

After feeding, lay the baby on your shoulder and let him belch. This prevents the baby from vomiting.

You should not feed your baby right just after intercourse. It affects the health of baby. If necessary, then squeeze some of the milk off and then feed.

If the baby behaves irritated all day, cries incessantly or if his weight seems less than normal, then check for some fault in your procedure of feeding.

When is breast feeding prohibited?

In the following situations, a mother should refrain from feeding:

1. When feeling emotions of anger, tension, sorrow, jealous, hatred or fear.

2. In an anxiety-ridden state.

3. In a state of extreme tiredness.

4. While being hungry.

5. In the fictitious condition.

6. In pregnancy (if a woman is already pregnant again, then feeding is prohibited for the health of mother and her unborn foetus.)

When to do when mother's milk is not available:

If mother's milk is not available, then it is better to give cow's milk, instead of any other artificial one. Boil the cow's milk well without mixing any water in it and use it at normal temperature. Use a bowl and spoon to feed the baby. Wash these utensils well after every use. If cow's milk is not available, then give buffalo's milk with ¼ water mixed in it. Goat milk after boiling is best for the baby.

External milk is given after boiling; this reduces vitamin-C in that. So those children which are given external milk should be also given one spoon of orange juice otherwise the child is prone to diseases.

If the baby gets ill while still being breast fed?

Perhaps by the mother's carelessness in diet, sleep, and life style etc. the infant might get sick. Treatment of the baby only while ignoring the mother's diet and health will not cure the baby and he will be sick from time to time. Alongside the child, the mother should also be treated.

Whether the baby is getting sufficient milk or not?

The mother cannot externally judge whether the baby has taken a sufficient amount of milk or not. But if the baby is sleeping properly, has sound health and remains good natured when awake and his weight is normal, then it is sure that he is getting sufficient milk for his nourishment.

If breast milk is not sufficient?

Breast milk formation is dependent on the rule of demand and supply. Formation depends on how often the mother feeds the baby.

If the breast milk is less not sufficient, the mother should take two litres of water, bread made of whole wheat flour and other carbohydrates. Fruits and vegetables are compulsory. Especially juicy fruits are a must.

During teething

If teething starts when the baby is still being breast fed, then give him/her only the mother's milk. But the diet of mother should be full of fruits, vegetables and milk. If the baby is to be weaned, then his food must contain excess of calcium.

Blood compression in nipples

Up to production of colostrum everything is normal, but when milk production starts, the nipples becomes hard and tight. It hurts even when touched. This condition normalizes in 24 to 48 hours. Feeding from such nipples may be painful for both mother and child. To get rid of problems during this phase adopt the following steps:

1. Before feeding, keep a lukewarm wet cloth on the nipples for some time. They will become soft.
2. Secrete some milk from both the nipples by pressing with your hands. This makes the nipple soft and the baby can grab them.
3. Don't stop feeding due to pain. The pain will increase if is the child feeds less.

Tonic for the breast feeding baby

If a baby gets the mother's milk and is healthy, then there is no need of tonic. But if the baby is suffering from stomach diseases and suffering from stomach pain, then he should be given gripe water of standard company.

Juice for a breast feeding baby

A baby which gets milk from a mother who is having a balanced diet needs no external food. But the juice of fresh fruits like orange, amla, tomato, sweet lemon can be given to a breast feeding baby and this can be continued afterwards too.

A bowl and spoon is better than a bottle

If giving external milk becomes necessary, then don't feed with a bottle. It is harmful for the health of the baby. It deteriorates teeth and possibility of diarrhoea increases.

Use a clean bowl and spoon for feeding the baby.

Registration of birth

Birth certificate is an important document. It must be prepared at the right time.

This is used in schools at the time of admission and in many other places.

For the registration of birth, some information is necessary.

Name of the baby
Place of birth
Date of birth
Father's/Mother's name

Full name and its spelling in all the places like School, Bank A/c, Saving Bonds etc. should be same.

Immunization

If the children are healthy, then from a young age, they can perform their responsibilities towards the family, society and the country by being fit physically, mentally and spiritually.

The environment is full of different type of disease causing bacteria/virus (microbes), but not everyone gets sick as different immune systems are present in our body to fight such diseases. This immunity may be inherent at birth. Other immunity power in the body may develop after birth. Immunity power developed after birth is different for different bacteria/viruses. Immunization for many different diseases has been discovered. There are still some more diseases for which scientists are still looking for preventive measures.

Combined vaccines have been developed now days which provides for prevention from more than one disease. Less number of immunizations means less pain to the baby, less trouble and less crying. The cost of immunization also decreases.

To get such various vaccines is called immunization.

Immunization of the baby is a must. Don't be careless about it. A child can be prevented from fatal and handicapping diseases by getting him proper immunization at a proper age. Get these vaccines even if the child has simple cough, cold and fever.

If any vaccine is missed at the scheduled time, then you must contact the health centre.

Age of baby	Vaccine name	Disease	Dose	Method
At the time of birth	B.C.G	Tuberculosis	One	Injection
	OPV	Polio	First	Oral Drops
	Hepatitis-B	Hepatitis-B	First	Injection
6 weeks	DPT (Diphtheria, Pertusis Tetanus)	Diphtheria, Pertusis, Tetanus	First	Injection
	OPV	Polio	Second	Oral drops
	Hepatitis-B	Hepatitis-B	Second	Injection
10 weeks	DPT	Diphtheria, pertusis, tetanus	Second	Injection
	OPV	Polio	Third	Oral drops
14 weeks	DPT	Diphtheria, pertusis, tetanus	Second	Injection
	OPV	Polio	Fourth	Oral drops

Age of baby	Vaccine name	Disease	Dose	Method
6-9 months	OPV	Polio	Fifth	Oral drops
	HBV	Hepatitis-B	Third	Injection
	Measles	Measles	One	Injection
1 year	Chickenpox	Chicken Pox	One	Injection
	Hepatitis-A	Hepatitis-A	First	Injection
15-18 months	DPT	Diphtheria, pertusis, tetanus	First Booster	Injection
	OPV	Polio	Sixth	Oral drops
	MMR	Measles, mumps, Rubella	First	Injection
	Hepatitis-A	Hepatitis-A	Second	Injection
2 years	Typhoid	Tyhoid	After every third year	Injection

Age of baby	Vaccine name	Disease	Dose	Method
5 years	DPT	Diphtheria, pertusis tetanus	Second Booster	Injection
	OPV	Polio	Seventh	Oral drops
10 years	TT	Tetanus	Third Booster	Injection
	Hepatitis-B	Hepatitis-B	Booster	Injection
15-16 Years	TT	Tetanus	Next Booster	Injection

Care of infant

To hold the baby in your lap, kissing him, to fondle, to make him play, to make him laugh, to tease him, to make him cry; all are different form of human love towards the infants.

Don't kiss the baby on his/her lips.

Prevent the baby from being exposed to too much open air and don't bring him under a fan or in front of a cooler. Lay him on a dry and soft bed. Be careful that he does not get cold.

Don't awake the baby in haste, awaken him slowly. Don't drag him towards you or don't throw him in the air. Never scold or rebuke the baby.

Always keep the baby away from windy places, direct sunlight, lightening, dark forests, lonely houses, storms, rain, bad places, dust and fumes etc.

The nursery of the baby should have dim light. Play melodious songs in a low volume, so that the baby becomes habituated to these things while sleeping.

If the baby has excessive hair on his body, then make a paste with gram flour (besan) and cream and rose water and apply on the body.

You can also make a roll of flour with cream or turmeric powder and rub the body of the baby with it in an opposite direction to the growth of hair. This will remove the hair from the skin.

After 2-3 months, smear the body of the baby daily with a paste of wheat flour, piyal seeds (chironji or charoli), yellow mustard powder and turmeric powder or any other traditional paste in the house. It will make the skin fair complexioned, shiny and soft.

Generally the head of babies are longer in shape rather than round. This is the effect of the exit of the baby from delivery canal. Mothers can make the head rounder by pressing it gently using mustard oil.

While lying on a single side (posture), the head of the baby becomes uneven. Hence use the pillow of mustard seeds (Raai).

The middle part skull of the baby (2-3 cm in diameter) remains pulpy. It may take 18 months to get hardened. Don't press it.

The baby's clothes should be cleaned and must be used after boiling as required. Change wet clothes immediately. Wash the dirty clothes immediately and get them dry in the sun.

To clean the eyes, nose and ears, wet cotton balls can be used.

Children enjoy bathing a lot. It is an important part of their routine work. In the lack of this, the body cannot be cleaned properly and they cannot attain good health.

Use baby soap or shampoo to bathe the baby.

Don't use much powder on the baby's skin. Powder particles are harmful for the lungs of the baby.

After bath, put a little kohl (kajal) on the eyes of the baby. Before putting it wash the hands well. Nail of the finger which is used for putting kajal should be properly cut.

Let the baby move all his body parts freely.

Diapers save the baby and clothes from getting wet. But use it carefully.

A wet diaper may cause many skin diseases to the baby.

Clean the urine and potty (faeces) of the baby properly.

Be careful while cleaning the potty of a baby girl. Don't touch the urine outlet as it may cause infection.

Try to establish a routine for the baby to use the potty. When the baby is small make a sound like 'soo-soo' to get him to urinate or toilet.

After cleaning the potty and nose of the baby, mother should wash her hands well.

Care of infant

Get the baby get used to air and sun positively, may be more or less according to the season.

When the baby is a few months old, take him for walks in open air in a baby carrier. Keep the baby away from any infected person.

If the baby has the habit of thumb sucking, in such cases he may get infections from dirty nails. The baby sometimes can scratch himself or others with long nails, so it is necessary to cut the nails of the baby from time to time. Cutting nails is much easier when the baby is sleeping.

Wash the hands and legs of the baby several times in a day but don't forget to wipe them dry, so that no fungal infection forms.

Get the baby cotton clothes and socks instead of synthetic ones.

The mother must wash her hands well before hand feeding the baby.

A child recognizes low sounds first, loud sounds later. A child will react first to the parent whose way of talking is quieter.

Don't ignore the baby when he is ill or wounded, however minor. This gives a secure feeling to the baby.

It is important to sympathize with and assure the baby, as the child can express his problems only by crying.

Massage of the baby

Gentle massages bring about physical, mental and emotional development in babies. It also enhances the blood circulatory, immune and digestive systems. Through touch and vibration during massages, the love and emotional relation between mother and child increases. Hence massages must be done by the mother or by someone closely related.

If the baby is anxious and crying, then a massage reduces his tension and irritation and he starts becoming less irritable.

One of the main uses of massages is that he gets a sound sleep. Leg massage of the baby gives him much relief and he sleeps well.

For massages, always use olive oil, coconut oil, sesame oil or almond oil.

A child who is physically weak from the time of birth can be given massages with cod liver oil.

Don't put oil in the ears and nose of the baby.

Massage the baby in a calm, warm and comfortable place. Don't put on the fan during this time.

Massages under the sun strengthen the body of the baby. It develops the bones and strengthens them, as vitamin-D is formed in sun rays. After a massage, keeping the baby in the sun for some time may also enable him to get a good amount of vitamin-D. But be careful that this activity is not done under the midday sun or when it is very hot.

Massage lightly as the baby has tender skin and his bones are also soft.

Every joint and bone should be massaged with a circular movement.

Get the baby do some exercise during the massage like moving legs and hands up and down etc, gently.

Massage the head of the baby with butter made from cow milk. It is believed to increase intelligence in the baby.

After the massage, let the baby play for some time in summer season and then get him bathed but in winter season, get the baby bathed immediately after the massage.

Every child wants love and attention from his mother and father. If a child gets love and attention from his parents then he will be same as his parents want him to be

Sleep of the baby

A mother is generally distressed when the baby does not sleep at night.

Generally we all have a sleep cycle according to which we go to bed and get up. We live according to it. The newly born baby takes some time to adopt this habit. So he has an irregular sleeping time. A baby takes around 6 weeks to adopt a regular routine and then the baby starts sleeping and waking at the right time.

Sound sleep results in good health. For babies too, sound sleep is good for their health and appropriate development.

For sound sleep — The sleeping room or nursery of the baby should be calm, quiet and clean with proper ventilation. It should have a dim light arrangement. The baby's clothes should be cleaned and loose for proper air circulation.

The baby is usually ready for sleep after play.

Wash his hands and legs before putting him to sleep.

Make him listen to lullabies (lori) etc. so that the baby goes to sleep peacefully.

Don't use medication to get the baby to sleep.

Don't let the baby sleep with anything in his mouth.

Don't cover the face of the baby.

Don't lay the baby on his stomach.

Don't awaken the sleeping baby unless it is urgently required.

Be cautious — In the beginning there is no problem in making the baby sleep.

Expected sleep

Age and condition	Daily
1 Month	22 Hours
2 Month	21.5 Hours
3 Month	21 Hours
4 Month	20 Hours
5 to 6 Month	19 Hours
1 to 2 year	16 Hours
3 to 5 year	11-13 Hours
5-12 year	9-11 Hours
Adolescent	9-10 Hours
Adult and Older	7-8 Hours

Crying (weeping) of the child

A baby can't speak so he starts crying when he is in trouble.

1. Hunger is usually the first cause of a baby crying. If the child is hungry he cries.
2. In the evening time, gas formation takes place in babies, so he might start crying. Usually the baby gets relief after the gas is passed out eventually. Give some gripe water to the baby to get rid of such problems.
3. Stomach pain and swelling in the stomach can also be the cause of the crying. Put a cold compress first, and then a hot one on the stomach. It brings the gas out.
4. A baby urinates and due to the discomfort of his wet clothes, may start crying. Change the clothes.
5. Sometimes insects may creep into the clothes and bite the baby which may make the baby cry. Check carefully for insects.

> **If a baby is crying without any reason and you lift him in your lap, then this makes the baby stubborn in future. He becomes habitual to get everything by crying, and then the parents get angry. Let the baby cry for some time. Crying is also important for his health.**

Parents' mutual affection — the best gift for baby

Mutual love of parents for each other, acts as a mirror for the baby. A baby observes the relation of his parents very closely and grows with those feelings in mind. This is the reason that the personality of a child is affected by this relationship and he becomes the same.

Effect of parents' tense relation on the baby:

Those children who grow up in a peaceful and gentle environment are often good natured and become optimistic in life. In contrast to this, those children who grow up in an environment where parents usually fight a lot grow up under a type of pressure. They find an inferiority complex in themselves and become pessimistic. Such children often do not develop a positive attitude towards life in the future. Such type of children grows up to have either, angry or quarrelsome personalities or they become excessively introverted and unable to stand up for themselves.

Children psychologically pay a heavy price when there are tense relations between parents. This affects the heart and mind of a child permanently and may require massive psychological help later on in life.

So, it is required that all parents should not disclose their dissidence in front of their children or never try to solve them overtly in the presence of their children, and try to solve them in private. It will be much better if parents do not hold back any bitter feelings in their hearts and try to solve the situation with mutual talk and understanding.

Parents' best gift for their children is that they live together in harmony with love and affection, so that the life of their children remains pleasant and peaceful.

If a wife sleeps on left side of the husband, then they are believed to the have same type of emotion and if it is opposite, then they are believed to have opposite feelings.

If both parents are working

If a working mother lives in a nuclear family, then problems arise as to who will look after the baby. In a joint family, such problems do not occur often.

There are also child care centre for working mothers. Some parents arrange for a maid. But if the parents are working then it is better that they make a shift wise duty so that they can look after the baby alternately.

If you cannot spend much time with your child, then spend quality time with him. It means, for the time that you are with him be with him fully. Don't be physically with the child and mentally somewhere else.

Play with him, tell him some stories and teach him good things. By doing this he will wait eagerly for your return home.

Don't bring office work back home. Don't vent your tension on your baby; otherwise he will come to think that it was better when the parents were not at home.

When a house maid is needed

When both the mother and father are working, then there is an urgent need for a house maid to look after the child. But we must take some precautions before appointing a maid.

1. First of all, get police verification of the house maid. Get her address, photo and information registered at a nearby police station. This will help ensure that the maid will behave appropriately and ensure the safety of your baby.

2. Get the house maid medically checked up from time to time. Be careful that she does not suffer from any infectious diseases. Children are very vulnerable and a house maid living with them must be free from infectious diseases.

3. The house maid must take bath every day. She must wear clean clothes everyday and keep her hands clean. Only then should she keep the baby on her lap or feed the child.

4. Instruct the maid to inform about the child's activity after every 1 or 2 hours by telephone. You should also call frequently. This makes the maid cautious not to neglect her duties because she knows that you may call any time.

5. A maid who is well fed might do her work more willingly. So it is better that you provide some light food or milk etc.

6. Appoint an older maid if possible, as on older woman might behave with more maturity.

7. Don't scold the maid without any reason. She will not take it well. After all she also has her own self respect. Tell her politely whatever you want to say. You can be firm but never harass or abuse the maid.

Sexual relations of parents v/s child

Don't have intercourse in front of the child even if he is only one month old.

Witnessing sexual relations between a mother and father leads to the rise of a violent feeling in the heart of children against their father. This feeling might manifest in a different form in the future. So in front of the children (at least when they are awake) don't make the foreplay activity. You might be thinking that the child does not understand your kissing, hugging, rubbing etc. this is your mistake. Though he does not know the meaning of these activities or could not express his reaction but he must understand the emotion. His tender mind gets affected by these activities. So parents should not have sexual relations till the baby goes in to sound sleep.

A child thinks you are ignoring him if you make him sleep alone. It affects him mentally.

Generally it is seen that woman are so busy with the child on getting used to motherhood, that the husband is ignored. This ignorance of husband deteriorates the relation between husband and wife.

If the mother sleep toward her son, the father may feel ignored, if the mother turns towards her husband, the child gets ignored. So if a woman sleeps on her back, she can't do it for an extended period of time. After some time, she has to turn towards husband or child. If the child sleeps in the middle then he gets the warmth of both the parents. This warmth will enhance your relation.

Family planning

In the present scenario, having too many children will be seen as being improvident. In a planned family, parents are happy and children get better chances of development.

There must be at least a three year difference between two siblings.

(Before the arrival of second child inform the elder child in such a manner that he becomes curious about the new arrival.)

The pregnancy in a woman of 20 to 30 years of age has higher chances of giving birth to a healthy child. It is better to be a mother during these ten years and use the future time to raise them well. The maximum of two children in a family is ideal. It will improve your health, you can provide better opportunities to your children and when you grow older your children will become self dependent. That time you can live your life in whatever relaxed way you wish to.

For a planned family, you can adopt any of the contraceptive methods like copper-T, condom, sterilization, oral pills etc.

But during lactation period, women should not use oral contraceptive pills.

For those women who have regular periods, one week (subtract three days from the middle day of the two consecutive periods and add three days) is considered to be unsafe (chances of conceiving).

Other means

1. Use of basil soup after every period can prevent an unwanted pregnancy.
2. Eating one clove daily can prevent pregnancy.
3. Neem (Margosa) oil also prevents pregnancy. This is the effective means of contraceptive.

'We Two Our One is Sufficient'

Alert parents now think that it is better to nourish one child with all comfort than to nourish two. It is better to nourish one child with best accomplishment and higher education to make him talented.

Diet of children

During childhood, the infant grows faster than at later stages. So it is important to pay much attention to the diet of children at this stage.

There is no doubt that mother's milk is best food for the baby, but as he grows up his requirement also increases.

So after the age of six months, in addition to mother's milk give him other kinds of milk, fruits, fruits juice, vegetables, vegetable juice etc.

Goat's milk is much better than cow's milk. Add large amount of water in the milk in beginning but when the child grows up reduce the quantity of water gradually.

Vitamin-C gets destroyed when the milk is boiled, so give one spoon of orange juice thrice a day. In lack of this, tomato juice can be given. If possible, one spoon of Amla juice is also sufficient.

Add honey or raisins (after grinding) in the milk but never add sugar to it.

Boil one cup of milk with half spoon of aniseed (saunf), it makes the milk light and digestible.

Boil the milk with pieces of one small cardamom; it makes the milk tasty and light. Instead of animal milk, soyabean milk, coconut milk, groundnut milk or sesame milk can be prepared.

After starting on milk, start giving fruits too. In starting, soft fruits like banana, papaya, sapota (chikoo) can be given but mash or crush them. Don't mash by hand but use a spoon for it. Fruits should be given only when the baby is hungry. Fruits should never be given when the child is not hungry, as child will not like new tastes when he is not hungry.

Make the child lick honey every day, it will make him healthy. It also helps in the teething process.

A child becomes healthy if he is made to lick potato juice mixed with honey.

Make the child drink tomato and carrot juice mixed with honey. It will act as a tonic.

Water of green gram (moong dal) or crushed green gram dal or vegetables soup is also beneficial.

Calcium and iron should be in sufficient amount in the child's food.

When the child is not interested in food or not taking milk or other food or he is sleeping then don't force him for the food.

Don't give cereals full of starch (like wheat and rice) till the teething process is completed, as the cereals do not get digested if not chewed well.

At the age of two, the child is weaned from breast milk and most of his/her teeth appear. Then, other different food items can be added to his diet which are light, easily digestible and nutritive. It includes fruits, vegetable, dry fruits and whole grains.

A child must be given moderately warm food. It should neither be too hot nor too cold. Also, don't give very hot food immediately after very cold food or vice versa. In the beginning, give in small quantities and then increase gradually.

Don't let the child have tea, coffee, a lot of salt, pepper, spices, chocolate, toffee, bread, biscuit, samosa, kachouri, sweets and namkeen etc. which are indigestible. All these items are stimulants. They don't get digested and produce a burning sensation in the stomach, which causes many diseases.

The habit of fast food and junk food make the child stubborn, temperamental and lazy.

Let the child take less salt from beginning so that they don't have to face disease in future. It is better to cook the

Diet of children

food by boiling or steaming or by roasting instead of frying. It is beneficial to use refined oil instead of butter.

When you start a solid diet for children, let them get the habit to eat by chewing well. It keeps the digestive system in a proper state, and avoids over eating. Fix the time for food and give the food at the right time. Solid food should be given thrice a day. Eating all the day is equivalent to inviting diseases.

To inculcate the habit of eating healthy food, do not bring indigestible food (fried, salty, sweets, preserved food etc.) into the house. Instead, make it normal to have digestible, nutritive and healthy food (fruits, dry fruits, sprouted pulses, juices, etc.) in the house.

Don't let unsuitable food be cooked in the house. Adopt the habit of simple food. If spicy items are cooked daily in your house, then you cannot adopt the habit of natural, simple food.

Every child is habituated to eating in times of natural hunger. But the parents or other family members teach them the habit of over eating by giving untimely food as temptation or as treats. This makes the child ill as eating food without being hungry is not conducive to health. When you force him to eat without feeling hungry, then he may start hating the food.

He will think that meal time is a burden and he may try to escape from it. Remember that no child likes to remain hungry. If he feels hungry, he will ask for food. And when the child eats while feeling hungry, then he will willingly eat everything and will eat even the simplest of food and will enjoy eating.

When the child is ill, give him only salad, fruits and juice.

All the family members should eat together and keep the T.V. off. Let the child adopt the habit of eating homemade food. Homemade food is fresh, clean and healthy.

There must be regularity in the food and life style of a child. In future, the child will continue to follow these habits which will keep him healthy and nourished throughout his life.

Those children who take natural food (seasonal fruits, vegetables, green leaves, salad, soaked dry fruits, sprouted cereals, fruits and vegetables juice etc.) hardly ever fall sick.

Note – For more information about uncooked food, read *Secrets of Natural Diet* by the same author.

'Children do not learn what we say.

Children learns what we do.

Malnutrition in children

Malnutrition in children is becoming a global problem. This is due to the lack of nutritious elements in the food being consumed.

Malnutrition is that condition in which the body does not get sufficient quantity of carbohydrates, proteins, fats, minerals, vitamins etc.

Up to the age of six months, mother's milk is sufficient to provide required nutrition to the baby.

After six month, the dietary needs of the child increases so he must be given extra nutrition.

Reason for Malnutrition

Insufficient supply of food.

Excessive junk food in which nutritious elements are few and only taste remains.

Excessive cooking, frying, roasting of food destroys the nutritious elements present in it.

Due to a weak digestive system, a child may suffer from malnutrition even after taking nutritious food.

If the food is not according to the children's taste then they will not eat food properly.

Those children who are fussy about their food also suffer from malnutrition. Such children do not get all nutritious elements.

Worms in the stomach.

Suffering from infectious or chronic diseases.

The mother was either too young in age or too matured when she was pregnant.

During pregnancy, if mother does not get appropriate food then it results in the birth of a weak baby.

If mother's milk is not sufficient, and the external milk is also not nutritious, then the possibility of malnutrition in a child increases.

Too many children and the absence of adequate gap between the two adjoining children, due to which no proper care is given to them also leads to malnutrition.

Effects of malnutrition

The mental and physical developmental rates of the child decreases while the chances of the child being mentally weak increases.

There is no continuous growth in the weight of the child, no remarkable feeling of hunger, a reluctance to participate in games and other physical activities, getting tired easily, feeling pain while sitting or standing, chronic constipation, cracks in the corners of the mouth and also some reddishness.

In the condition of malnutrition, cells in the body weaken slowly and as a result, they stop working. So, infectious diseases like cholera, tuberculosis and other internal diseases like diarrhoea, pneumonia etc. may attack easily.

Malnutrition weakens the body and it may lead to night blindness, beriberi, scurvy, rickets, teeth problem, osteoporosis, and constipation and constant burning sensations, irritation and other diseases.

Hands and legs of the children become very weak and due to liver enlargement, the abdomen appears swollen.

Fat content in the body of the child decreases, which makes the skin loose, wrinkled and cheeks shrinks and flesh from the buttocks hang. The body becomes a frame of bones (skeleton). The face appears like that of an old man.

Diseases caused by malnutrition

Lack of protein causes retarded development, lack of vitamin-A causes night blindness, lack of vitamin-B causes beriberi, lack of vitamin-C causes scurvy, lack of vitamin-D causes rickets, lack of iodine causes goiter, lack of iron causes anaemia.

Prevention from malnutrition

During pregnancy and after delivery, the mother should get a full nutritious diet, so that there will be sufficient milk in her breasts for her child.

Ensure that the mother's milk is sufficient for child. Check whether the child keeps crying constantly.

After six months, gradually start giving extra food to the baby. A one year old baby can eat almost everything.

A growing child needs fresh digestible food instead of artificial vitamin pills and tonics.

Pay attention to the likes and dislikes of children while serving them food, so that they can relish a full diet.

Food should be of various types so that all important minerals, vitamins, proteins, carbohydrates and fats etc. can be given in a balanced form to the child.

Use uncooked/raw food (Seasonal fruits, vegetables and juice etc.) in plenty.

It is a cure for worms in the stomach.

Don't let the baby eat mud/soil and other unhygienic things.

Have proper family planning so that one can afford to give the child proper and adequate nourishment.

Thumb sucking by children

This activity generally starts when the child puts his thumb in his mouth when he is crying and he starts sucking it. He stops crying. This activity may provide some relief to the harried mother and she may become careless about her child's habit. Some mothers even use artificial suckers to calm the crying child.

Those children who don't get milk and food in time seem to adopt this bad habit of thumb sucking.

Disadvantages of sucker (pacifier) or thumb sucking

It reduces the appetite. The child has lesser demand for food and it may affect their health badly.

The teeth start growing in an outward direction or there is a possibility of them being slant. Even the lips become deformed. The child inculcates the habit of keeping the mouth constantly open and it also affects the shape of the face.

The thumb which is being sucked becomes tender in comparison to the other one, which will have adverse effects in future.

While sucking the thumb, dust or other foreign particles enter the body which may affect health badly.

To get the child to get rid of this habit of thumb sucking

Give food and milk to the baby at right time. If you notice that the child is sucking his thumb, then take the thumb out and make him drink milk.

Don't let him keep up with his bad habit.

Some mothers apply pastes of chilli powder and other strong-tasting items like salt and neem oil to get rid of this habit. This is also not good as it may be hazardous to his health.

Some parents slap and scold their kids for thumb sucking. This is also not encouraged as it hurts their self respect. They may continue this habit as a means of showing wilful disobedience.

So behave carefully under these circumstances.

When the baby tries to put his thumb in his mouth, give him some attractive thing like toys to divert his mind from it.

Try to get rid of this habit patiently and gently, otherwise the baby might start acting even more will fully.

The habit generally starts when there is an inadequate amount of calcium in the mother's milk. Give the mother a calcium-rich diet which includes items like milk, oranges, wheat bran, green leafy vegetables and sesame etc.

Teething

Generally there are no teeth in the mouth of babies at the time of birth but the process of teeth forming inside the gums start by the fifth month of pregnancy.

By the age of six months, growing of teeth starts which generally goes for about 2 years. These newly formed teeth are called primary teeth.

If teething process does not start even after six months, then it is assumed that there must be some deficiency of calcium in the child.

First, generally, two teeth from lower gums appear and then followed by two teeth from the upper gums.

Primary teeth are generally 20 in number.

The primary teeth start breaking off between the ages of 4 to 6. Then, again a new set of teeth appears. In the sixth year, there are about 8 new teeth formed. At a younger age, usually there are 32 teeth formed which are not permanent.

Wisdom teeth generally appear at the age of 18 or so and sometimes do not appear at all.

At the time of teething, a child must be given food rich in calcium. If the baby is still being breast fed, then the mother's diet must be rich in calcium.

At the time of teething, some children suffer from diseases of the stomach, fever, lethargy, general weakness, irritation, anxiety, etc, while many children don't have any visible symptoms.

During teething, the gums may feel itchy or ticklish due to which the child want to chew something. This is why the baby may put everything he touches in his mouth. It may lead to ingestion of many unsuitable items, resulting in the stomach getting infected and the child suffering from diarrhoea.

Teething

Give a hygienic soft rubber toy or carrot etc. to the child to chew. It will help in teething.

Give clean peels of pomegranate to the baby as chewing them will help in teething.

Let the baby lick the juice of pomegranate mixed with basil juice as it helps in teething easily and prevents diarrhoea.

Make the baby drink one spoon of water after boiling it with one spoon of aniseed four times a day, it reduces problems during teething.

During teething, massage the gums with amla juice as this also makes the teething process easier.

100 gm pineapple juice with a little lemon juice is also helpful.

During teething, give the child water from a white bottle after drying it out thoroughly in the sun as it helps in the teething process.

Massage the gums of baby with roasted grounded borax (sohaga).

Care of child's teeth

Don't make the baby sleep with the milk bottle in his mouth. Don't let him eat chocolate. If he eats then wash the mouth immediately after. Washing the mouth immediately after eating anything is necessary.

Don't let the baby suck his thumb as, it deteriorates the teeth.

Start brushing habit from the age of about one and half years of age.

Food rich in calcium, phosphorus, vitamin-C and D is beneficial in the process of forming permanent healthy teeth. You must include sufficient green vegetables, fruits and honey in his diet.

Consult with the dentist from time to time.

Activities of the infant

First month
The child generally sleeps on his back, looks here and there by turning his eyes, sometimes smiles after looking at the mother. The child starts crying if he is hungry or feeling any discomfort. Seeing, listening and tasting ability develops. His hands and legs show some movement, but he cannot control the movement of his neck. So it is necessary to put a hand on the nape of the neck while lifting the baby. Most of the time, the infant spends the time sleeping after feeding. Many times, it is seen that the child sleeps the whole day and stays awake at night.

Second month
Starts somewhat recognizing his mother/primary caretaker. He starts moving his head on hearing some sounds and shows vague expressions of happiness on hearing music and seeing recognizable faces. He seems to smile back when people smile at him and takes interest in his surrounding environment. He starts to make incoherent noises.
The baby seems to be listening if we talk to him.

Third month
The baby can usually control his head around the 3rd month, if he is lying on his stomach. He starts laughing and tries to look at and tries to grasp anything within his reach.
Starts making noises on seeing his parents or any familiar person and looks like he is trying to listen carefully.

Activities of the infant

Fourth month

The baby starts controlling his body movements much better. He can turn in the direction of sound and can turn his sleeping side. He seems more observant and alert than before and seems to be aware of his surroundings. He tries to stretch out his hands towards toys when shown to him and tries to grasp things within reach.

Fifth month

In the fifth month, usually the baby can control his neck and head quite well. He can even sit for some time with the help of pillows or other external support. Now he starts recognizing more familiar people. He may sometimes start crying on seeing strangers.

Six month

May be able to start sitting by himself; can grasp things firmly in his hands.

Seventh month

May start moving his head indicating displeasure.
 Shows his liking and disliking towards food fed to him. May make incoherent noises which sounds like he is trying to talk. Starts crying and may throw tantrums over trifle things.

Eighth month

Many children at this age can start crawling on their abdomen and knees. They can sit without any help. They may even be able to or try to, say easy words like 'Mama', 'Dada', etc. The child is usually able to recognize oneself in the mirror by this age.
 The child may even display tantrums by throwing things.

Ninth month

This is the time when the baby may start crawling on his knees. He often gets the meaning of simple words by this age. Starting crying if scolded or spoken to harshly is a common reaction.

Tenth month

Most babies can usually stand using chairs or sofas for support and may try to take steps forward. The child can exhibit common and simple gestures like 'waving bye-bye', etc.

Eleventh month

The baby starts crying or sobbing if denied for something. Has the habit of sitting a lot. Usually can stand without any external help and advanced learners may be able to start speaking a little. (Don't make the baby stand forcibly as when he is ready, he can do it himself)

Twelfth month

Most children can usually drink by themselves from a cup (with handles). They can also usually hold a biscuit and eat by themselves. He may be able to speak two or three words. He may be able to say out aloud, half/ incomplete names to the things he is familiar with, like milk, water, biscuit etc.

The baby at this age usually understands simple sentences and instructions. He may be able to walk with support and enjoys it. Tricks of sleight of the hand, etc, and playing with the spoon while feeding him will amuse him.

Thirteenth month

The baby's fingers flexibility and limbs mobility becomes more steady and sure.

Activities of the infant

Fourteenth month
The baby laughs, smiles and is able to show affectionate gestures like giving kisses etc. if taught to do so.

Fifteenth month
Babies can usually start walking minimal distances steadily, with firm steps by this age.

Sixteenth month
Can usually walk fast or run but still not very steadily.

Seventeenth month
Can stack up toys, one on top of the other and can amuse himself by throwing things to the floor and picking them up.

Can open boxes and cartons, if strong enough. Curiosity at this age can make him acquire the habit of putting his finger into holes. He can now hold a cup properly.

One and half year
Listens and understands simple sentences, recognizes the parts of the body if taught and speaks with half-completed words. The baby can play a lot by himself or with others. He likes to scatter, collect and pick up toys. The baby can learn to use a spoon decently well.

One and half year to two year
Can speak simple sentences of two or three words with more confidence. (Parents should speak in clear tone to the baby, this will increase his confidence.)

The child can usually climb up or down the stairs if supported by someone else. By this age, if he is taught well, he can indicate when he feels the need to use the toilet.

Two years

The child may be able to attempt putting on or taking off his shoes. He can draw a straight line with a pencil. He can learn to play music from this age.

Two and half year

The child can differentiate between different colours and speak more articulately, specially the language spoken the most in the home environment.

Two and half to three years

Most children by this age are quite well versed at speaking simple sentences continuously and might have the habit of repeating themselves. He can draw circles and crosses with a pencil. Gradually becomes more capable at attempts to put on or take off his clothes.

Three years

He can jump and play by himself quite well and is usually capable of climbing up and down the stairs without support. Children of this age are usually capable of riding three-tire bicycles and can play and get well along with other children. He can express his emotions and are usually capable of drawing simple figures like square, triangle, etc.

He can recognize the names of his immediate family members and can usually tell the name of other different figures. He can count up to ten and can learn nursery rhymes if taught.

Children's temperament

During this young age, the child is like soft clay which can be moulded in any way. The education which is given to a child in the first three or four years of his life becomes an important part of his nature and will stay with him throughout his life.

For example, if he does not like sweetened milk, he can be taught to drink. Or he may not like salty things but he can be gradually taught to tolerate it.

Fear — Do not frighten the baby unnecessarily, as this fear may become a permanent part of his psyche and he may grow up to be a faint-hearted individual.

Anger — When the child is hindered in getting his way, then he will become upset. Don't forbid the baby from doing anything but divert his mind from something he wants that you deem unsuitable. For example, if he picks up something which he shouldn't, then the parents should give him something else and exchange them, so that he does not feel deprived. He gets the feeling that something better is given to him instead of feeling that he is being deprived of something.

Happiness — He is happy on getting things he is interested in.

Love — Demonstrate your love for him physically like giving hug and gentle pats and also, look at him with love and indulgence. A child who is showered with the right kind of love and affection grows up as a better adjusted, emotionally rounded out individual.

In the beginning, babies are completely dependent on the parent, physically and emotionally. They need a lot of attention, so give him a lot of love to forge strong bonds and tell him simple, easy stories of morality and ethics.

Children's nature

A baby generally cannot sit still even for a minute. His hands, legs, eyes, nose, ears and all his senses are always alert. The baby is always curious about his surroundings. He wants to experience everything by himself, so he runs and jumps as well as climbs up and down the stairs continuously and keeps on picking up many different things all the time.

A normal, healthy child is usually very active and will always want to be engaged in some sort of activity, unless he is ill.

Children are normally very active, with over flowing energy and a need to be involved in physical activity almost all the time. Parents should ensure that the child is involved in some sort of constructive activity all the time to burn off his excess energy. If not, the child might find other destructive outlets for his boundless energy.

Children are naturally eager for new toys and to search out new ways to amuse themselves. They want to do everything in their own way. So they amuse themselves with all the things in the house. This is a part of their development. Don't suppress this part of their nature as long as it is not hazardous to their health. All these things are helpful in their development. It increases their way of thinking and understanding and the power of their imagination.

Threatening and beating children or forbidding them from doing anything leads to suppression of talent and dwarfing their creative side. If this keeps up, and the child is not allowed to do anything he desires, it might make him introverted, awkward in social settings, lacking in self esteem and withdrawn.

Children's nature

Some activities are given below that a child can enjoy and do easily.

1. All children do their personal work with great interest. Generally, parents think that the children are weak and so they wait on them hand and foot. This is a major mistake. Show the children the way to do the work and supervise them from a distance while the children go about the work of bathing themselves, combing their hair, buttoning and unbuttoning and wearing clothes, polishing shoes, cleaning up after themselves, putting things back where they found them, doing light laundry, washing utensils, serving food etc.

2. Children like wooden blocks and card paper a lot. With these, they use their creativity to build and create what is in their imagination. Children also love playing with empty match boxes, using them like wooden blocks.

3. Mud and sand is often a favourite plaything for children. They love playing in the sand and creating sand castles and digging pits etc.

4. Children love to draw pictures of the things surrounding them like animals, birds, insects and sometimes even people. Don't make fun of their drawings. Always encourage them and let them develop their talent.

5. Give the child a notebook so that he can make a scrap book. Let him paste pictures from old newspapers and magazines. Give him glue stick and a dustbin to throw the garbage.

6. Children are eager to make new things. Encourage them to make flower garlands, pearls garlands, toys, spools, kites, envelops etc. from old cards and papers.

7. Children generally like to play with colourful pieces of cloth. They can amuse themselves by folding the handkerchief and then unfolding it. They also like to

combine and decorate them. The pieces of cloth you give to them should be small in size.

9. Children also like to separate mixed items. Give them a bowl full of different kinds of beads in different colours and shapes. You will see that they amuse themselves by differentiating the different beads into different groups and again mixing them. This increases their distinguishing and classification powers.

10. Children like to make toys from mouldable material like clay. This keeps them occupied and they enjoy it. Taking from their daily experience, they try to make various fruits, animals, utensils, aeroplanes, houses etc.

There are endless activities suitable for different ages and these are all good for the child's overall development.

If the child is looking at you in the process of making something, then it is clear that he wants your help.

Many children usually do some appreciable activity in school or around the neighbourhood .If there is something else that they are interested in, they will say it to you, tentatively or articulately and you should listen to them carefully, and answer them accordingly so that they will be satisfied with the answer. If they want to show interest in any of activity like painting, embroidery, knitting, etc, then you must praise their creativity and show active interest in them. Parents' approval is very important to the development of the child's self esteem and confidence

Safety measures to adopt around children

Children's curiosity can often be a headache for parents as often this leads them to do reckless things, unmindful of consequences and they don't know what they are doing. Nobody likes accidents, least of all with young children involved.

So be careful with the child all the time. Keep an alert eye on the child at all times, especially, when the baby starts to crawl or learn to walk.

Keep electrical appliances like table fan, iron, heater etc. away from the reach of children. Switch them on only when there is somebody in the room to keep an eye on the baby. Use safety caps or tape on the electric points which are within the reach of the child.

Keep all the brittle/easily breakable items away from the reach of children.

Children often like to stay attached to or in the proximity of their mothers. Hence there is high possibility of them putting their hands on or into anything the mother has on hand. So keep all potentially harmful things like hot tea, milk, etc. out of the child's reach.

Keep strong chemicals like soap, detergent, phenyl, bleaching powder, insecticides, etc. away from the reach of children. Also keep medicines away from the reach of children.

Children have the habit of putting everything they see into their mouths. This is potentially very hazardous as the child might choke on anything. So don't keep small ornaments, coins, pins, button, etc. in open spaces that the child can easily reach.

Don't keep furniture with sharp corners. Children may collide with them and hurt themselves. If unavoidable, baby-proof them by attaching padding on the sharp corners.

Give the children toys which are suitable for their age. The toys should not be pointed or have sharp edges.

Helpful toys in the development of children

By playing with toys, a child becomes active. It enhances his imagination power. He develops a healthy mind which increases his mental ability. Good toys always enhance the working ability, working skill and creativity of a child.

For children, whether boys or girls, good toys suitable for different age groups, are available in the market. Before buying the toys, see the quality and material used. It must be made of nonbreakable material. It should not have sharp edges which can harm the baby. Toys should be made of high grade plastic which is not harmful. Do not be swayed by toys which are pretty but might potentially cause harm

Don't purchase those toys which put a negative effect on the mind of the child or develop violent tendencies in him. Keep in mind the age and requirements of the child while buying toys for him.

0-3 Months

The senses of a baby from birth to 3 months of age are limited to listening and seeing. At this age, the baby likes colourful toys and toys which make sounds and can attract his attention.

3-6 Months

By this age, teething process usually starts in children. So there is much irritation in his gums. He will want to chew everything he can put his hands on. So, give him hygienic and safe rubber or plastic toys which are generally called tethers.

6-9 Months

Children generally can start sitting by this age. He tries to walk on his knees. Give him dolls, walking toys and colourful balls. These toys attract the attention of the baby and he will try to walk on his knees to catch the toys.

9-12 Months

The child tries to hold the things around him or to walk by using the support of things around him. At this age he will need a four wheel walker. In addition to this, now, as his mind becomes sharper, give him toys to help him distinguish between different colours as well as building blocks etc.

1-2 Years

The child starts walking at the age of one year. He tries to apply his own mind. At this time, turn his mind to one-line story books which have many colourful pictures. Tell him stories by showing different pictures.

Give him unbreakable creative blocks so that he can try to make something new.

Give him beginner books to distinguish between different colours, fruits, vegetables, animals, birds etc.

Children generally like music a lot. Make them listen to songs rhymes.

2-3 Years

Children at this age like to take things apart and put them back together. Children's minds are very creative. To enhance their creativity, give them such toys which can be taken apart and put back together, like wooden blocks, dolls with clothes and jewellery, balls, trains set etc. so that they can play with them according to their imagination and create new things.

Multipurpose toys enhance the imagination power of the children and encourage them to make new things.

3-4 Year

Children of this age are more mischievous. They like jumping from heights or sometimes try to climb high places.

They hang onto a support with both hands or play by lying on the ground. To divert them from mischievous activities, give them problem solving toys, wooden puzzles, blocks, etc. Also give them nontoxic washable crayons, marker, paint brush, finger paint in various colours, plain papers for drawing and painting. Teach them to fill colour in the dotted pictures. Also encourage them to make different dotted pictures.

For physical exercise, different size of balls to be played by hands and legs are beneficial to them.

4-5 Years

This age requires more care for the child. They want to experiment with everything according to them. They enjoy sitting, playing and sharing toys with their friends. Some new creative toys like blocks, small cars, building sets, furniture, kitchen set, chairs, different clothes, building blocks which can be used to make different buildings should be given to them to enhance their imagination. Give them drawing and painting items, music instruments like mouth organ, musical guitar, key board, reading books, CD, DVD etc.

Note – Now a days it is the time of computer game and play station. But psychologist says that if the child play with the traditional toys then his development gets better. Many psychologists says that if they play the traditional game then the ability of leadership rises in the children. In electronic games and computer games, they don't have to think much, neither they have to use their imagination power much. To adopt such type of game the creative activity in children decreases. Also the speaking ability in the children weakens.

The first five years of a child is creative. In this period the mind of a child is like a sponge, he has the ability to pick up and absorb more and more informations. 85% development of the child mind happens during this period.

For mental and physical development of the children it is necessary to go out and play. So parents have to make a balance between the indoor game and outdoor game. Develop the habit of playing children outside the house from the beginning. Take him to the garden to make him play balls, plastic disc, bat ball, etc. regularly.

> **Those children who are nourished well do the great jobs of the universe.**

Importance of playing

It has been proved scientifically that playing is beneficial, not only physical development but also for mental and social development. According to physicians, those children who don't have time to play outdoors often suffer from bone diseases in the future. So encourage the child to play, indoors and outdoors. Fix a specific time for games. Outdoor games develop the child physically whereas indoor games develop their intellect and increase their mental power. So encourage the child to play both indoor and outdoor games. If possible, play together with them. You can accompany them in games such as badminton, etc, and indoor games like carrom board, ludo and chess. If possible, give them training by a trained coach if they show increasing aptitude for a specific game. Apart from a good formal education, extracurricular activities are also important for overall development of the child.

Games are important while the child is at a growing age. Generally, parents think that games are for only for infants. Many parents ban games for the sake of education of their offspring. This is absolutely wrong.

> **There are many yogic activities which develop emotional and creative feelings in the children. Yoga increases self confidence, self control and self-consciousness in them.**

If the child is lethargic

If the child is not active like his peers, don't immediately accuse him of laziness. It is better to consult a doctor first to rule out any health reasons.

Reasons for lethargy

1. If the mother has not taken nutritious food at the time of pregnancy.
2. At the beginning of pregnancy, if the mother suffers from German measles or Rubella type of infections, then the baby will be born with infection. Due to this, the baby becomes mentally weak or suffers from glaucoma.
3. During delivery if there is any trouble, like no proper supply of oxygen to the baby during delivery or any other reason, the baby remains lazy.
4. If the baby is suffering from congenital diseases like respiratory disease, rickets, heart disease, etc.
5. If the baby does not get a balanced diet, then immunity power does not develop properly and the child will be plagued often by continuous diarrhoea, fever or anaemia.

What to do – If a disease can be cured, then get it cured. And if due to malnutrition, the baby is weak then get a diet chart for the baby and give him food accordingly. In the mean time, continue giving encouragement to the child. Love him

If the child is lethargic

and try to keep the house environment calm, so that he can be cured in time.

> **The child recognizes his surroundings and the people around him quickly and makes his temper as of his family. So, mother and father should keep their best character so that their child can be of that nature.**

Physical growth of children

1. Normal height and weight of children upto age of 4 years.

	Boys		Girls	
Age	Height (cm)	Weight (K.gm.)	Height (cm)	Weight (K.gm.)
At birth	50.0	3.0	50.0	3.0
Upto 3 months	56.0	4.5	55.0	4.0
4-6 months	62.5	6.5	61.0	5.5
7-9 months	65.0	7.0	64.5	6.0
10-11 months	69.5	7.5	66.5	6.5
1 year	74.0	8.5	72.5	8.0
2 year	81.5	10.0	80.0	9.5
3 year	89.0	12.0	87.0	11.0
4 year	96.0	13.5	94.5	13.0

2. Standard, minimum and maximum weight chart as per height of 5-17 years children.

Note – For girls, count the weight of 2 cm less from the given height.

Age 5 to 7 Years							
Height (cm)	Min. (K.gm.)	Normal (K.gm.)	Max. (K.gm.)	Height (cm)	Min. (K.gm.)	Normal (K.gm.)	Max. K.gm.)
94	11.9	13.7	18.8	114	16.2	18.5	25.4
96	12.3	14.0	19.3	116	16.8	19.2	26.4
98	12.5	14.3	19.7	118	17.4	19.9	27.4
100	12.8	14.6	20.0	120	18.0	20.6	28.3
102	13.1	15.0	20.6	122	18.6	21.3	29.3
104	13.5	15.4	21.2	124	19.3	22.0	30.3
106	13.9	15.9	21.9	126	20.0	22.8	31.4
108	14.4	16.5	22.7	128	20.7	23.7	32.6
110	15.0	17.1	23.5	130	21.5	24.6	33.8
112	15.6	17.8	24.5				

Physical growth of children

Age 8 to 9 Year				Age 10 Year			
Height (cm)	Min. (K.gm.)	Normal (K.gm)	Max. (K.gm.)	Height (cm)	Min. (K.gm.)	Normal (K.gm)	Max. K.gm.)
114	16.1	18.4	25.3	114	16.6	19.0	26.1
116	16.8	19.2	26.4	116	17.2	19.6	27.0
118	17.5	20.0	27.5	118	17.6	20.2	27.8
120	18.0	20.6	28.3	120	18.2	20.8	28.6
122	18.6	21.2	29.1	122	19.1	21.8	30.0
124	19.3	22.0	30.2	124	19.6	22.4	30.8
126	20.0	22.8	31.2	126	20.3	23.2	31.9
128	20.7	23.6	32.4	128	21.2	24.2	33.3
130	21.7	24.8	34.1	130	22.1	25.2	34.6
132	22.6	25.8	35.4	132	23.1	26.4	36.3
134	23.7	27.0	37.1	134	23.7	27.0	37.1
136	24.2	27.6	37.9	136	24.5	28.0	38.5
138	24.9	28.4	39.0	138	25.6	29.2	40.1
140	25.6	29.2	40.1	140	26.5	30.2	41.5
142	26.5	30.2	41.5	142	27.3	31.2	42.9
144	27.5	31.4	43.1	144	28.2	32.2	44.2
146	28.7	32.8	45.1	146	29.3	33.4	45.9
148	29.8	34.0	46.7	148	30.1	34.4	47.3
150	30.9	35.2	48.3	150	31.0	35.4	48.6
152	32.0	36.4	49.9	152	32.4	37.0	50.8

Age 11 Year							
Height (cm)	Min. (K.gm.)	Normal (K.gm)	Max. (Kgm.)	Height (cm)	Min. (K.gm.)	Normal (K.gm)	Max. K.gm.)
124	19.6	22.4	30.8	144	28.7	32.8	45.1
126	20.5	23.4	32.2	146	29.6	33.8	46.4
128	21.4	24.4	33.5	148	30.0	35.0	48.1
130	22.1	25.2	34.6	150	31.7	36.2	49.7
132	23.1	26.4	36.3	152	32.3	37.4	51.4
134	24.0	27.4	37.6	154	34.2	39.0	53.6
136	24.9	28.4	39.0	156	35.2	40.2	55.2
138	25.8	29.4	40.4	158	36.4	41.6	57.2
140	26.8	30.6	42.0	160	37.0	43.0	59.1
142	27.0	31.6	43.6	162	37.6	44.4	61.0

Age 12 Year				Age 13 Year			
Height (cm)	Min. (K.gm.)	Normal (K.gm)	Max. (K.gm.)	Height (cm)	Min. (K.gm.)	Normal (K.gm)	Max. K.gm.)
126	20.5	23.4	32.2	126	20.8	23.8	32.5
128	21.5	24.6	33.8	128	21.7	24.8	34.0
130	22.5	25.8	35.4	130	22.6	25.8	35.4
132	23.5	26.8	36.6	132	23.5	26.8	36.8
134	24.4	27.3	38.2	134	24.4	27.8	38.2
136	25.4	29.0	39.8	136	25.4	29.0	39.8
138	26.3	30.0	41.2	138	26.3	30.0	41.2
140	27.2	31.0	42.6	140	27.2	31.0	42.6
142	28.0	32.0	44.0	142	28.0	32.0	44.0
144	29.1	33.2	45.6	144	29.1	33.2	45.6
146	30.1	34.6	47.5	146	30.3	34.6	47.5
148	31.4	35.8	49.2	148	31.4	35.0	49.0
150	32.2	36.8	50.6	150	32.2	36.8	50.6
152	33.3	38.0	52.2	152	33.6	38.4	52.8
154	34.5	39.4	54.1	154	34.9	39.8	54.6
156	35.6	40.7	55.9	156	36.1	41.2	56.6
158	36.8	42.0	57.7	158	37.8	42.6	58.5
160	38.2	43.6	59.9	160	38.5	44.0	60.5
162	39.4	45.0	61.8	162	39.9	45.5	62.5
164	40.6	46.4	63.7	164	41.0	46.8	64.3
166	41.8	47.8	65.6	166	42.4	48.4	66.5
168	43.0	49.2	67.5	168	44.1	50.3	69.1
170	44.2	50.6	69.4	170	45.8	52.2	71.7

Age 14 Year				Age 15 Year			
Height (cm)	Min. (K.gm.)	Normal (K.gm)	Max. (K.gm.)	Height (cm)	Min. (K.gm.)	Normal (K.gm)	Max. K.gm.)
136	25.7	29.4	40.5	136	26.8	30.5	41.3
138	26.8	30.4	41.8	138	27.6	31.6	42.7
140	27.5	31.4	43.1	140	28.4	32.5	43.9
142	28.6	32.6	44.8	142	29.3	33.5	45.2

Physical growth of children

Age 14 Year				Age 15 Year			
Height (cm)	Min. (K.gm.)	Normal (K.gm)	Max. (K.gm.)	Height (cm)	Min. (K.gm.)	Normal (K.gm)	Max. (K.gm.)
144	29.8	34.0	46.7	144	30.6	35.0	47.9
146	30.8	35.2	48.4	146	31.5	36.0	48.6
148	31.9	36.3	50.0	148	32.6	37.2	50.2
149	32.4	37.0	50.8	149	32.9	37.6	50.8
150	32.9	37.6	51.7	150	33.3	38.0	51.3
151	33.6	38.4	52.8	151	34.0	38.8	52.4
152	34.3	39.2	53.9	152	34.7	39.6	53.5
153	35.0	40.0	55.0	153	35.3	40.3	54.4
154	35.7	40.7	56.1	154	35.9	41.1	55.4
155	36.3	41.4	56.9	155	36.6	41.8	58.4
156	36.8	42.0	57.7	156	37.3	42.6	57.5
157	37.5	42.8	58.8	157	37.8	43.2	58.3
158	38.2	43.5	59.9	158	38.5	44.0	59.4
159	38.8	44.2	60.9	159	39.2	44.8	60.5
160	39.4	45.0	61.8	160	39.7	45.4	61.3
161	40.0	45.6	62.7	161	40.4	46.2	62.4
162	40.5	46.3	63.5	162	41.1	47.0	63.5
163	41.3	47.2	64.8	163	42.0	48.0	64.8
164	42.0	48.0	66.0	164	42.9	49.0	66.2
165	42.8	48.8	67.2	165	43.7	49.9	67.4
166	43.5	49.6	68.3	166	44.5	50.8	68.6
167	44.2	50.8	69.0	167	45.0	51.4	69.7
168	44.9	51.2	70.3	168	45.5	52.0	70.2
169	45.7	51.8	71.6	169	46.3	52.7	71.2
170	46.4	52.4	72.8	170	46.7	53.4	72.1
172	47.7	54.4	74.7	172	48.0	54.8	74.0
174	48.9	55.8	76.7	174	49.2	56.2	75.9
176	51.1	57.2	78.6	176	50.4	57.6	77.9
178	51.4	58.6	80.7	178	51.4	59.0	79.7
180	52.7	60.2	82.7	180	53.0	60.6	81.8

Age 16 Year				Age 17 Year			
Height (cm)	Min. (K.gm.)	Normal (K.gm)	Max. (K.gm.)	Height (cm)	Min. (K.gm.)	Normal (K.gm)	Max. (K.gm.)
136	28.0	32.0	43.2	136	30.8	35.2	47.5
138	28.9	33.0	44.6	138	31.5	35.0	48.6
140	29.8	34.0	45.9	140	32.2	36.8	49.7
142	30.6	35.0	47.3	142	32.9	37.6	50.8
144	31.5	36.0	48.6	144	33.8	38.4	51.8
146	32.6	37.2	50.2	146	34.3	39.2	52.9
148	33.7	38.5	52.0	148	35.0	40.0	54.0
149	34.1	39.0	52.7	149	35.4	40.4	54.5
150	34.6	49.5	53.3	150	35.7	40.8	55.1
151	35.1	40.1	54.1	151	36.2	41.4	55.9
152	35.5	40.6	54.8	152	36.8	42.0	56.7
153	36.1	41.3	56.6	153	37.3	42.6	57.6
154	36.8	42.0	56.7	154	37.7	43.0	58.1
155	37.3	42.6	57.5	155	38.2	43.7	59.0
156	38.0	43.4	58.6	156	38.9	44.5	60.1
157	38.5	44.0	59.4	157	39.7	45.4	61.2
158	39.1	44.7	60.3	158	40.4	46.2	62.4
159	39.7	45.4	61.3	159	40.9	46.7	63.0
160	40.7	45.8	61.8	160	41.1	47.0	63.5
161	40.3	46.6	62.8	161	41.7	47.6	64.3
162	41.3	47.2	63.7	162	42.2	48.2	65.1
163	42.1	48.1	64.9	163	42.9	49.0	66.2
164	42.9	49.0	66.2	164	43.3	49.5	66.8
165	43.7	49.9	67.4	165	43.8	50.1	67.6
166	43.7	50.8	68.6	166	44.5	50.9	68.7
167	45.0	51.4	69.4	167	45.3	51.8	69.9
168	45.5	52.0	70.2	168	45.9	52.3	70.9
169	46.3	52.7	71.2	169	46.6	53.3	72.0
170	46.7	53.4	72.1	170	47.3	54.0	72.9
172	48.0	54.8	74.0	172	48.4	55.3	74.7
174	49.2	56.2	75.9	174	49.6	56.7	76.5
176	50.6	57.8	78.0	176	50.9	58.2	78.5
178	52.1	59.5	80.3	178	52.1	59.5	80.3
180	53.5	61.1	82.5	180	53.5	61.1	82.5

Physical growth of children

Note – In the same age group of male and female children, male children are seen to grow faster than females in terms of weight. The weight of the child increases regularly if they are given proper nutritious food. Such children will be active, fit, and cheerful and will be healthy, physically and mentally.

For increasing height

Include more soyabean milk, sesame milk, green leafy vegetables, fruits and salad in the child's diet. Try to get the child to do tadasana, suptapavan-muktasana, uddiyanbandh, nadishodhan pranayama.

Regular massage especially of the back bone.

Put a mark on a wall and get the child try to touch it by standing on tiptoes. If he can touch that mark, then increase the mark level on height.

If you are able to teach the child to swim then go for swimming.

Spend most of your time in open air.

Indications of disease through infant's signals

Even the slightest irresponsible behaviour towards an infant can lead to some minor or major problems. The child can neither speak nor can he tell about his suffering to anyone. He can only convey his discomfort by crying loudly.

The way birds and animals use allusive language to express themselves, similarly a child also adopts allusive language to express his agony. The need is that the guardian understands the child's allusive language.

The sick child has dirty tongue brown in colour and some lines are formed on it, he has problem while passing urine and stool, he does not get proper sleep and starts screaming and shouting in sleep, his growth gets stagnant, body weight decreases and appetite becomes nil.

- If a child touches some part of the body while crying or cries when someone else touches that part then it should be noted that the child has problem in that part.
- If the child takes his hand to the head again and again but is unable to straighten the head then he might be having a headache. On having pain, the child keeps his eyes also closed.
- If while crying a child raises his stomach by lifting his back then it indicates his stomach pain.
- If a child bites the breast while having milk then he is either sick or his teeth has started coming out.
- A child having worms in his stomach gnashes his teeth while sleeping, scratches the nose and rubs his urinal and

stool area. If there is saliva coming from a child's mouth then one must know that definitely the child has worms in his stomach.

- While being breast fed if the child often leaves the breast for breathing then it indicates cold. During cold the child breathes from mouth instead of nose.
- If a child's temperature has risen and his nerve runs fast then it indicates fever. In fever the child's face too becomes red.
- If along with fever the child starts sneezing and his face becomes red then they are pre-indications of measles and chicken pox.
- If a child makes out noise from the mouth, it indicates the occurrence of throat or breathing related disease.
- If a child teeth come out one by one then he is suffering from rickets.
- Opening the mouth and taking out the tongue repeatedly indicates that the child is thirsty.
- If a child breathes heavily and his ribs and chest also show forceful movements then the child is suffering from cold and congestion.
- If a child has pain in ears he repeatedly tries to put his finger in the ears.
- Repeated mouth breathing along with rustling sound from chest and bloating of nostrils are signs of pneumonia.
- Pain in chest, lungs, ribs or crying while coughing indicates pneumonia.
- If the child is lazily lying with closed eyes then he has some internal problem.
- If the child touches his urinal organ repeatedly then it can be known that his urine has got blocked.

- Repeated clutching of fist and nibbling of lips indicates his heart pain. In this situation the child's heartbeat becomes fast.
- If the child's body become stiff like a bow that mean tetanus is having its effect.
- Sudden occurrence of itching feeling indicates that the child is sick.

Natural treatments for common diseases in children

A sick child needs rest, physical affection and extra care. During this time the child will want more attention from his parents. A sick child can be entertained inside the house or on the lawns and up on the terrace under supervision.

In those households where care is given only to the health of child and not to the health of the mother, the child is found to be frequently sick. This is because a child initially gets his nutrition from the mother's milk. If the mother is not well, then how can we concentrate only on the health of the child.

Give fresh fruits, vegetables and milk to the mother during this period. In addition to these, give trifla, basil, neem etc. which act as blood purifiers, so that the mother's milk will be free from any abnormality. Use enema to clean the stomach.

Use mosquito net if mosquitoes are there. Use a clean sheet and change it frequently.

Try to keep the sick child happy and busy. It increases the possibility of a speedy recovery.

Stop giving the child unnatural and synthetic food items and start natural foods like fruits juice etc. Let the child get air and sun properly. Be kind and indulge the child up to a limit.

Note – Most parents get children to fear the doctor to make them eat food they don't like or to make them drink milk. For example, they say "drink milk; otherwise the doctor will come and give an injection" or something similar. It creates a phobia in the mind of children towards the doctor. He starts being afraid while going to the doctor. This makes it difficult for the doctor to examine the child. So try not to do this even by mistake.

Ejaculation of milk (Vomiting)

Vomiting after feeding is a common complaint in children. It is due to accumulation of air in the stomach. The mother should feed the baby in a sitting position, and the head of the baby should be upright. After feeding, put the baby on the shoulder and don't leave him lying down. Pat him on his back for 20 minutes so that he can belch.

When the mother observes that the child is vomiting the milk instead of drinking, then she should understand that her baby has been overfed. If possible, give one spoon of orange juice to the baby before feeding for better digestion of milk.

If the baby vomits too frequently, then give amla and black raisin water with half a spoon of honey.

Excessive crying

There may be many reasons for excessive crying, such as hunger, wet clothes due to urination, too-tight clothing or feeling of excessive warmth or cold. But there may also be some health related reasons and by curing them, the baby can be prevented from crying excessively.

Abdominal pain

In abdominal pain, the feet of the baby remain cold. The pain occurs frequently. The baby cries loudly when it hurts. He bends his legs in an upward direction. Use hot and cold compress over the abdomen and put asafoetida (Heeng) paste around his navel. It will give a great relief to the baby.

Diseases related to digestion

Give grounded harad, mixed with one celery seed (Ajwain) and small fried borax (Sohaga approximately equal to 2 pieces of rice in quantity) all mixed in water.

Dysentery

If the child suffers continuous loose motion, give mint juice thrice a day.

Constipation

Use mud paste over the abdomen and give fruits and vegetables juices. If the child is a little older, give him pulpy fruits and vegetables. If a breast feeding baby suffers from constipation, give him one or two spoons of amaranth (choulaee) juice.

Cold and cough

To prevent children from cold and cough, give them nutmeg (Jaayphal) ground in water.

If the child is suffering from cold and cough, then give him lemon water with honey and vegetable soups.

Give hot and cold fomentation for fifteen minutes on the back and abdomen (hot for two minutes and cold for one minute alternately). Tie the compress (wet sheet inside and dry woollen on outside) on the back and chest for 45 minutes to one hour.

Grind cloves or aniseed (sounf) in honey and get it licked by the baby thrice a day. Give water from an orange coloured bottle which has been kept the whole day in the sun, three to four times a day according to age.

In cough and cold, give hot fomentation on the palm and feet of the baby.

Don't give any medicine to eat or to apply for babies below two year of age.

Nasal congestion

Clean the nose by dropping in one or two drops of salt water inside the nostrils.

Increased respiration

Use mud pack over the ribs at intervals of three hours. It gives relief. Mix celery seeds (ajwain) in pure ghee and massage it over the chest.

Mix mustard oil in onion juice, heat it till it is lukewarm and massage the child. This gives relief to the child.

Development of children

Feed the child fresh leaves of basil and a little black pepper powder with honey or massage the chest with sesame oil of red bottle processed (basked) in the sun and let him bask in sun light through a red transparent paper to give relief in pneumonia.

Enlargement of liver

The liver of a breast fed baby is enlarged when his/her mother uses ghee (fat), maida or sugar in excess. For this, more care should be given to the mother's health than the baby's treatment. For this problem, the mother should be given milk, fruits and vegetables in excess.

Ear ache

Use hot and cold fomentation near the ear.

Boils and pimples

Generally, boils and pimples appear on the body of children. Use pastes of green coriander leaves on them. It gives relief.

Grind the peel of margosa (neem) and use this paste on the skin. It also cures boils and pimples.

Ulcer in the mouth

The only reason for it is toxicity of the mother's milk or the child is possibly suffering from constipation. The mother should take green vegetables, salad, fruits and milk in excess in her diet.

Grind harad in water or in gulab jal (rose water), give it to the baby. Use mud packs on the abdomen (mud packs are very effective). Give fresh water frequently. Give juice of oranges or sweet lemon. Give water of curdled milk mixed with honey.

Tonsillitis

If the baby is feeding on mother's milk then the mother should take fruits and green vegetables so that the blood gets purified. If the baby has been weaned off breast milk, then give him fruits and vegetables only and use enema to clean the stomach.

Apply lemon juice on the tonsils. If the baby is a little older, then make a gargle of warm lemon water. Do hot and cold fomentation of the throat for fifteen minutes. Wrap wet sheet packs round the neck at night.

Massage between the thumb and adjoining finger of hands and legs for two minutes.

Note – Tonsils should not be cut out by operation unless it is absolutely necessary as it may cause infection, memory loss, impotency, epilepsy and obesity in the future.

Fever

Don't let the fever rise above 104°F. The best way to reduce the temperature of the baby is to lightly wash the body with a sponge or wet cloth.

Give vegetable soups and luke warm water to the child when he is suffering from fever and then start orange juice. When the fever is normal and the tongue is clear, then give him fruits and milk. If fruits and milk are not easily available then give a balanced common diet.

Prolapse of rectum (Kanch)

Wash the anus with alum water on prolapse of rectum.

Mumps

Mostly children of the age group 4-15 suffer from this disease. Give enema with lemon mixed with luke warm water. Give hot and cold fomentation (2 minutes hot, 1 minutes cold alternately, four rounds at a time) on the affected part twice a day. Use wet mud packs on the affected part.

Include a lot of juices, vegetable soup and fruits in the diet.

Prevention from heat wave

Give sponge baths to the baby twice a day. Give him a bath in water of the same temperature as that of the body. Let him play in open spaces in the morning.

In the morning, let him sit in the sun initially for five minutes and then increase it gradually to 30 minutes.

The baby should get fresh air; his/her bed should be in a mildly cold room. The room should have proper ventilation.

Worms in intestine

If a child has worms in his/her intestine then he becomes weak and irritant.

Children may have pin worms in their anus which bites in the anus, so the child cries and cannot sleep. Soak a cotton ball in kerosene oil and put it in the child's anus. This kills the worms and the child gets relief. Pumping a little lime water in the anus also gives relief from pin worms.

If a child of the age group of 1 to 3 years suffers from pin worm, then boil radish and mix rock salt in it. Strain it and give two spoons of it to the baby in the morning. Worms will be killed and will come out.

Give amla juice to the baby for a week daily, one to two spoons or according to age.

Give cooked tomato with rock salt and black pepper on it. Give three or four times a day, water from a green bottle which has been basked in the sun to the baby.

The worms get destroyed if the baby is given jaggery with raw turmeric. If stomach pain is there due to worms, then give bitter gourd (karela) juice mixed with turmeric powder.

Give onion juice if worms are there in the intestine.

Eating basil seed also kills the intestinal worms.

Give enema of boiled neem leaves or garlic water twice daily.

Dullness

If the child's mind is not acting according to his age, then the reason behind it may be constipation, excessive use of sugar, some kind of mental fear etc.

Use mud packs on the abdomen. Give enema. Give sitz bath in the morning. Next time give hip bath. Wrap wet bandage over the stomach and waist.

Include salads in his diet. Use more vegetables. Give breakfast of soaked black raisins and figs in the morning.

Arrange playing items. Make the habit of going to botanical parks. Massage the back bone. Make him happy. Don't get angry at him.

Aniseed powder with honey enhances the mental power of children. Make a flow of water on the head. Make the sun rays fall on the head through a blue piece of glass.

Bed wetting

Mostly those children who are scared and are scolded urinate in sleep.

Don't scold or beat the child. Don't humiliate him as he is not doing it consciously.

Make the habit of making the child urinate before going to bed.

Give 20 raisins and two walnuts to the child to eat at bed time.

Boil dry dates with milk and the child drink it. It will take effect within a few days.

Give one comfit (laddoo) of sesame and jaggery or of sesame and dates every day and then give one glass of milk mixed with honey to drink.

Give one spoonful of honey to the child at night before sleeping.

Stop giving sweets. Extract the seeds from black raisins and add the same quantity of black pepper to it. Make him eat two or three such black raisins in the morning.

To clean the stomach, use mud packs on the stomach. Use enema for four days or give triphala powder. Give the child a hip bath. Give hot and cold fomentation on the backbone. Let the child lie in the sun and massage the backbone. In the evening time, give sitz bath. Give water from a green bottle basked in sun rays, four times daily.

When the child goes to bed, say in his ear seven times "Go to urine if you feel so" and mention his name.

The problem of increasing obesity in children

Problem of obesity in children is increasing day by day which increases the possibility of physical weakness, diabetes in early age, hypertension etc. in children.

Firstly, pay attention to the eating habits of children. To change the habit of children, it is necessary for the parents to change their habits first.

Tell him about the harmful effect of junk food, packed food, prepared food bought from the market as well as the food items made from white flour (maida), sugar, ghee and oil. Encourage him to avoid such food. Don't bring aerated drinks into your house. Coconut water can be a substitute for that. Roti instead of bread, steamed food instead of fried food, nuts instead of snacks can be preferred. Make the habit of eating fruits or salads before any meal.

Let children exercise for one hour daily. Make time in your busy schedule to take the children to a nearby park and play with them.

Discuss about the health in your family. The type of food and the type of routine which can make you and your child healthy, all these you must not only discuss it but must adopt it yourself first.

Care of the eyes

The eyes are the most delicate and sensitive organs. A little mistake can affect it badly. So to maintain proper eye sight and beauty of the eyes, they must be looked after carefully.

From the moment he is young, the child should take a diet rich in vitamin-A, B and C. Wheat grass juice is best for it. Make the child avoid looking at direct sunlight up to the age of four years.

If the eyes are red, excessive waste appears in the eyes, continuous lacrimations (tears) or squint is observed in the eyes of the child, consult an eye specialist immediately.

Eye care at a higher age

Immediately after waking up, fill the mouth with clean water and sprinkle water on both the eyes. Also wash them properly while bathing.

Don't put hot water over the head and don't wash the eyes in hot water.

Massage the soles of both feet with mustard oil.

See the sun with closed eyes for at least five minutes.

Walk bare footed on the green grass in open air in the mornings. This also enhances the eye sight.

For the cleanliness of eyes, put one or two drops of rose water (gulab jal) in the eyes.

Dissolving one small spoon of triphala in one glass of clean water and washing the eyes with it is also beneficial for the eyes.

Jalneti is also beneficial for the eyes.

As much as possible, protect the eyes from the direct heat of sun, dust, smoke and strong winds.

Care of the eyes

Sleeping late at night and awakening after sunrise is harmful for the eyes. So make the habit of going to the bed early and rising early in the morning.

If you have to stay up till late at night, then keep drinking a glass of water at the interval of one hour.

The book should be at a distance of 30 cm from the eyes while reading. The light should come from the back side of left shoulder while reading. To give rest to your eyes, close them occasionally for one minute or concentrate your sight at a thing far away. The light should neither be dim nor highly intense. Don't read while lying down, it gives tension to the eyes.

The page of the paper should not be so glossy or shiny that it affects the eyes.

The eyes also get affected when you read books of small prints or when you do intricate embroidery for a long time.

Don't stare at shiny objects or far away objects.

If it is time to sleep and your eyes are tired, then it is not good to remain awake.

If you have to work on a computer for a long time, then give the eyes rest by pressing your palms on them with light pressure.

Eyes also get affected by sitting in front the T.V. screen for a longer time. The rays coming out from the screen harms the eyes. It is better to sit at a sufficient distance from the T.V. screen. Minimum distance must be six time the length of T.V.

To remove burning sensations, pain and tiredness of the eyes, put a cold wet cloth pack on the eyes for ten minutes in the morning and evening.

Constipation also affects the eyes. So to remove or to prevent constipation, drink a glass of luke warm water in which the juice of one lemon is mixed.

If you have to work for a long time then you must give rest to the eyes for 5-10 minutes after the interval of one and half hour or two hour.

Smoking and drinking alcohol also affects the eyes.

Mental tension also increases eye diseases.

Irregularity in food, malnutrition also affects the sight of the eyes.

Minimise the use of red chili powder, sour and spicy food. Take fruits, sprouts, juices etc. in plenty.

Wash the eyes at least twice a day with cold water.

Use homemade kajal on the eyes while going to sleep.

Wash it in morning with a wet cloth.

Take one or two spoons of triphala powder with water or honey while going to sleep daily.

To maintain beauty of the eyes and to prevent eye sight from weakness, it is necessary to have proper sleep.

Open and close your eyes about 25 times daily as it increases the blood circulation and enhances the eye sight.

Do eye exercises (palming, shifting etc.) daily.

Enhancing resistance power (immunity)

Children fall ill due to weak immunity. Enhance the immunity of your child in a natural way.

For increasing immunity

The food should be nutritious, balanced and digestive.

Balanced diet should consist of all food items like fruits, vegetables, cereals, seeds (giri), milk products, etc. Different varieties of item should be taken from each category. (For example, different types of fruits and vegetables).

For a good immune system, neither over eating nor under eating is good.

Vitamin-A (milk, yellow fruits, vegetables etc.), Vitamin-C (orange, grapes, pineapple, amla etc.), Vitamin-E (sprouted grains, apple, vegetables etc.) are beneficial for the enhancement of the immunity. Give amla to the children from beginning.

Children should take plenty of water and juices every day but in summer, fluids intake should be more.

Teach the child to wash hands properly many times a day, especially before eating and after using the toilet.

Give the child boiled margosa (neem) leaves-water bath after every 15 days (fortnightly).

Ensure that your baby gets fresh air and opportunity for play and exercise outside the house.

Watching T.V. should be limited. Instead of that, it is better to encourage them to go outside and play.

If your child is sick, then minimise the food and drinks with sugar in them. Sugar destroys immunity.

Physical and mental stress also weakens the immune system.

Problems of children

If the child sleeps during the day and stays awake at night

Firstly, parents should have patience in this condition, and then gradually they should try to change the routine of the child. For that, change the sleeping habit of the child gradually. Let him sleep less during day. It does not mean that you don't allow him to sleep at all in the daytime, but allow him to sleep only for some time in the day so that he may not get tired. Napping for a bit in the day time is beneficial for the child.

If the child doesn't want to get down from the mother's lap

Make the child sit on the ground and put plenty of toys before him. The child will be happy on seeing the toys and start sitting down.

When the child does not take to new people

Let the child go sit in others' (new people's) lap. Don't lose patience when the child cries. If he cries, try to calm him without picking him up from the person's lap. This will change his habit and he will learn to mix with others also.

If the child eats soil

If the child is young, then take care of him yourself. When the child tries to eat soil, divert his mind and put a tablet of calcium in his mouth. With that, he will forget soil eating.

Give mango seed powder with water and the child will leave the habit of eating soil.

If the child doesn't like to share

A child must learn to share because those children, who do not learn to share their things with other people, often find themselves friendless and alone. Such children cannot adjust themselves anywhere, which leads to much maladjustment.

Parents should teach their children that sharing their things with others is a good habit. Everyone praises the child who has a sharing nature. When you give your things to others, only then others will give you their things.

If the child starts walking late

If the child does not start walking at the normal walking age or walks on his knees, then massage his feet with good oil and pay attention to his diet so that he can get full nourishment. Give him milk, ghee, curd, fruits and vegetables regularly. Still if he is unable to walk then take him to a specialist doctor to know find out the problem and if there is a way to solve it.

If the child is unaware of potty manners

If the child is unaware of potty manners or deliberately goes for toilet here and there, then the situation becomes humiliating and troublesome.

To avoid such conditions, parents are required to tell the child from beginning that there is a separate place for potty and urine. Also tell them that when they are outside and feel like using the toilet, then they should inform the parents first and the parents can do something about it. Parents should remain patient if the child goes for potty here and there. Potty training takes time. Don't beat or scold the child but make him understand that it is not a good habit and he should not do it in future.

If the child can't speak

If the child starts uttering one or two words then be sure that he will start speaking sooner or later. In India, it is often seen that the child starts speaking earlier as compared to children elsewhere. The main reason behind it is that in India parents are seen to interact more with the child. To interact with him is necessary.

If the child works with his left hand

This in itself is not a major problem. But if the parent wishes to make the child use his right hand more, give something attractive in the left hand of the child at the time of meals. Also give something in the left hand when the child is doing some work. Doing this gradually will reduce his dependence on his left hand.

If the child stammers

The children start stammering if they are mentally weak or scared or scolded. For this, the diet and routine of the children should be natural; they should be given sun baths and the back bone should be massaged daily and constantly reassurance and kindness must be shown to the child.

Encourage the morale of the child who is stammering. Don't provoke or rebuke him.

Develop an open atmosphere for the child at home so that he does not hesitate in voicing his emotions to family members.

Get him to stand in front of the mirror and make him practice talking to himself.

Get the child involved in games, music, scouting, yoga or martial arts classes.

Ask him to participate in different social functions. Get him introduced with people and encourage him to talk to them.

Give hot and cold baths, and put mud packs and sheet packs on the throat. Massage the backbone and put wet compress over the backbone. Give sitz bath.

Autism

Autism is the disorder of the inability to communicate verbally or otherwise with other people.

Symptoms

- Many a times the child is not able to answer any question.
- He avoids eye contact.
- He himself keeps busy in his own work.
- He keeps playing with a single toy unlike most children who tire of toys easily.
- He may be hyperactive.
- He exhibits repetitive behaviour.
- He keeps moving both hands continuously.
- To see a particular light or to hold a particular thing firmly is the main symptom of autism.

It is of two types:

1. Infantile Autism — It is found in the children of age group 6 months to 1 year.
2. Childhood autism — It is found in children above one year of age. Many times people assume such children as dull. But there are differences. Sometimes extraordinary abilities and talents are seen in such autism affected children.

He may be skilled in solving the mathematical problems or puzzles. It has also been seen in the children affected by this disease that they can calculate and show you the calendar for the next two years and they can stand first or second in the class in terms of academic performance.

Treatment – If a very young child is suffering from autism, it can be controlled within three years by giving a special therapy. If such a child is brought into the main stream of the society and send to school for normal child they will learn to adapt eventually, to a high degree, but perhaps a full cure is not entirely possible.

Medium or high autism takes even more time to be controlled up to a certain limit. Such a child's mind has been affected and their social circle becomes limited. Such children can be helped by speech therapy, behavioural therapy, play therapy etc.

When the child is shy (diffident)

Such a child does not take interest in anything. He doesn't play with other children nor go for walks and even slinks away at the sight of the guest who comes to the house.

How can such a child succeed if he has the same behaviour in future?

There may be many reasons behind this habit. A child is not timid by birth. Very few children show such behaviour by birth. Most children become timid by the influence of their parents or atmosphere around them.

Sometimes it is seen that parents scold the child needlessly over trifle thing-. "don't do this, don't do that", "don't come here, don't go there", "don't play with this child", "your stomach will get upset by eating this", "don't speak like this," etc. etc.

Repeated interrogating and interference makes the child timid. He will have the constant fear in his mind about whether the thing he is doing is right or wrong. Thus, the child becomes diffident.

Be positive instead of being negative with the child- such as giving him options to do any other work instead of simply denying him what he wants.

In many houses, the atmosphere is such that people hesitate in every matter. They even can't laugh openly while talking to anybody due to some culture of discipline and propriety. Small children get immediately affected by it. They do as they see and later, it becomes their habit.

Generally, it is seen that when some adults are discussing over a matter and if a child interrupts them in middle or suggests something, then they scold the child and tell him to be quiet. This hurts the child and if it happens repeatedly, the child hesitates to sit along with his parents and others.

So, whenever the child asks questions, it is better to pacify the curiosity of the child by explaining things to him in the right way.

If the child remains silent, then we can start some topic in which the child takes interest and feels his worth. If it is so, the child will behave as usual and it will help to terminate his diffident tendency.

Friendly relations with the child can often give him full mental development. There may not be another better way than it especially in order to make the child more socially adept. The parent's friendly company is better than the company of questionable peers. They can ask any question directly to the parents and when they get the answer, it will have a healthy effect on their minds. Then the topic of inferiority complex will never arise.

If the child talks to his family members openly, then he will have no hesitation in facing peers and guests or talking in a disciplined and polite manner.

When the child is stubborn (obstinate)

Many children become stubborn due to excess affection and indulgence from their parents. They get whatever they want. This habit becomes dangerous a lot of times. Such children remain stubborn for the rest of their lives. Many a times the child cries to make you agree to his desire. If you deny, then he may bang his head on the floor. If you deny further then he may lie down on the floor. Then you get tired and accept his desire and promise to fulfil that. From here on, the child understands that crying gives nothing but everything can be made by lying down on the floor. Then he starts doing that constantly.

In the same way, if you deny something initially and later on due to his stubborn behaviour you agree for that, then the child becomes stubborn later.

What to do?

It is wrong to say yes for everything, but it is also not good to say no for everything. The things which are necessary must be agreed to by you. If some of his desire/ requirements are met then he will not be so stubborn. For example, sometimes purchase toys and make him eat things that he wants.

If you have denied something to the child, then you must tell him the reason. You should remain strict on your stand whatever the child does (sulking, crying etc.).

Be careful that once if you have said 'no' to something then don't concede it due his persistence. If he understands the fact that parents' 'yes' or 'no' is final, then he will never insist.

Both parents should have the same opinion on it. It should never be that one says 'no' and other says 'yes' to that. If one is too strict and other, too soft then the child takes advantage of it. The thing which you (the parents) don't like should be denied clearly by both the parents simultaneously.

If other members are there in the house, then they should also not take the side of the child.

If the child throws tantrums, then also you should not shout at him. Control your anger but don't show yourself to be alright with the tantrum-throwing. Otherwise this will make the child think that his parents are not affected when he throws tantrums. Later on when his anger cools down, sit him down and talk; make him understand that his behaviour has hurt you very much and all his friends and teacher will think him to be a bad person.

Accept this fact regarding persistence that a cold iron cut the hot iron.

When the child is hyperactive

A child who doesn't pay attention to any work, and is talkative, aggressive, irritant, and over active for his own age, then he might be suffering from ADHD (Attention Deficit Hyperactivity Disorder).

Such children are hard to handle. They spread dirt in a few minutes, immediately start fighting and persist over trifle things. In school they also fight with their fellow students. They cannot complete any game and they have problems in maintaining friendships.

General characters of the child suffering from ADHD

- Lack of attention.
- Can't concentrate on long texts given in the school curriculum.
- High chances of mistake due to carelessness.
- Can't follow instructions in school.
- Often loses things.
- Forgetful nature in daily activities.
- Often persistent shaking seen in the hands and legs.
- Gets distressed in situations where there is no need for stress.
- Having problems in playing games requiring sitting at ease.
- Feeling restlessness or having unquiet behaviour.

- Speaking more than need.
- Hurry to answer before listening to the question.
- To feel troubled while waiting for his turn.
- Often interferes in others' work in school or in the house.

To help such children
Make them count all those works which they are yet to complete e.g. making the bed, removing the dirty clothes, and keeping his toys back at their right places etc. This type of instruction may produce good results.

You should also reward them on the completion of the work that they have been assigned to. You can reward them by letting them play or listen to stories, etc.

There is one another way to help encourage such children Your saying of words such as "you will feel happy if you ask for this toy rather than snatch it" can change them more. These children try to change their behaviour as they get a positive response from you.

Keep them busy mentally using works like reading, solving puzzles etc. In their diet, include various coloured fruits, vegetables, soyabean, walnut etc. Don't give them tea, coffee, fast food etc. Try to take them to yoga and meditation classes.

All research has come to the conclusion that the behaviour of a child depends on what type of atmosphere he gets around himself during his childhood and what was the attitude of his parents towards him.

Recognizing mental tension in children

If the childhood does not pass with joy and amusement, it cannot be called as 'childhood'. The smile on the faces of children can lighten up any dull atmosphere. But with time, life has become so burdened that even the childhood is not untouched by it. Mental tension has snatched the smile from the faces of many children.

The fast-paced life has increased tension in adults but it is a matter of sorrow and wonder that tension is being found even in children. Due to this cause, many diseases are developing. This problem is seen to be worse in urban children.

These days, tension has reached such high limits that cases of running away from homes or committing suicide is increasing rapidly.

Adults can articulate their tension and problems verbally but children cannot do that. They try to articulate their problems through their behaviour. The main symptoms of mental tension are often, uncontrollable unruly behavioural traits like- breaking/throwing things, suddenly getting angry over trifle things etc.

Does your child get irritated too often, doesn't seem to hear you or play with you or even to talk to you? Does he show no interest in things like food or company of other children? Does he always seem distressed or afraid? Are you observing sudden strange changes in his behaviour?

If it is so, then you must be alert. These may be symptoms of childhood depression. Often most parents ignore them, considering as them as 'misbehaviour'.

The word 'depression' is mostly used for adults, but it sometimes also affects children. Even children of three or four years of age may get affected by it.

If a child is suffering from depression, then he might possibly miss all the social activities necessary for his full development. If the problem is not given due attention in time, he might have problems forming emotional attachments in the future.

This kind of problem can be easily taken care of but parents need to understand their problems and take proper steps to help them.

Reason of tension in children

The children of those women who were in tension or depression during pregnancy may also develop depression.

Scolding and beating the child unnecessarily also increases mental tension in the child.

Nowadays, due to the highly competitive environment, parents expect children to be good at everything and excel all the time. This puts excess pressure on children and stresses them out.

These days, most parents are also so busy that they often do not have enough time for their children's problems. So often, children cannot express them freely. They feel suffocated from the inside. They think that nobody understands them or wants to listen to them.

Those children, who don't get proper guidance or live in an unsuitable environment, get easily affected by depression. It shows in their behaviour throughout their life.

Loneliness may be fatal for children. Parents' love and attention is very important for the development of children.

Fights or tension in the house, death of near ones, settling into new places, parents' divorce, academic stress or failure are often the causes of depression in children.

If a child is mistreated, emotionally or physically, then also it affects the child adversely.

Symptoms of mental tension in children

- Remaining quiet or looking sad all the time.
- Get bored even with his favourite things or games.
- Behaving pessimistically.
- Crying over trifle things, chewing on nails or lips etc.
- Not speaking properly.
- Feeling guilty even if the mistake is not committed by him.
- Being excessively emotional.
- Being constantly angry and getting irritated easily.
- Not watching T.V or listening to music or other activities. Being always self absorbed and introverted.
- Not taking interest in studies and games.
- Facing problems concentrating.
- Eating very excess or very less.
- Trying to run away from home a lot.
- Showing suicidal tendencies.
- Bed wetting.
- Extreme needy or clingy behaviour.
- Showing extreme anti-social behaviour without reason.

Effects of tension in children

Although stress is a mental disease, yet it can also affect the physical development of the child. As in—

- Frequent pain in the abdomen of such children.
- Dysentery in children.

- Impaired physical growth.
- The child may be too thin or bordering on obese.

Preventing stress in children

- For parents who have a single child, sometimes, for that child loneliness is a burden. Parents should give extra time to such a child.
- Talk to your children and know what is going through their minds and listen to what they're saying.
- Show or tell them how to get rid of their problems. Tell them to write down their problems and encourage them to fight against those problems instead of giving in.
- Parents should not quarrel in the presence of children. Do not tell your personal problems to your children.
- Whenever children do some good work, you must appreciate and encourage them and show physical affection like hugs too.
- Parents should give full attention to the child while spending time with him. It enhances friendly relations between parents and the child.
- Whenever you see that the child is in bad mood or looking sad, try to make the general mood lighter. Children feel stressed in a tense atmosphere.
- Don't put excessive burden of other works on children when they get back from school. Don't press them to always top the class in every activity. It keeps the child tense about his activities and he also remains afraid of not being successful and disappointing you, which he does not want at all.
- Take advice from an expert for problems which you cannot solve by yourself.

To help the child out of depression

In the treatment of child depression, sensitivity is a must. Parents' behaviour and the environment around the child is much more crucial than medicine. Adopt friendly nature with child than dictatorial. This kind of problem takes time to get cured, but with efforts in right direction, he gets well soon.

Try to spend more time with the child during his depression. Give him love and affection and don't make him feel that he is suffering from any kind of disease.

Encourage the child to pursue activities which he enjoys.

Parents should openly talk to the child. Try to understand him without questioning him too much.

After listening to their problems, don't dismiss the problem as small or useless. Make them believe that you are taking their problem seriously. Let them feel reassured that you are with them and that they will be able to get rid of their problems. Make them understand that it is normal to have problems and they're not alone in it.

Don't force the child to accept your opinion but make him understand why you are giving such an opinion and ask him to consider.

Take the child for a trip outside and introduce him to new things and take him to different places. This will introduce fresh ideas in his mind and it will help in reducing the tension.

Let him feel reassured that everything is well with him and the family and that he is safe and all of you are paying attention to him.

During depression, there may be hormonal imbalance in the child, so pay special attention to his diet.

Children will learn as they see

It is said that the nature of the parents affects the child the most. Parents, generally being the primary care givers, play the main role in moulding a child's behaviour, more than any other person. Generally good nature in the parents begets similar behaviour in the offspring. The type of impression shown to the child when he is young will play a very important role in the future development of his personality. Children follow parents' behaviour very closely.

So, parents should behave in the same way as they expect from their child.

Whatever you want to teach them, you should show them how to do first by action. They will learn that immediately. For example, if you want your children to wish you in the morning, then at first you should start wishing them or perhaps your own parents.

If you don't want your child to smoke then you should also not smoke. If you want your child to be polite and talk in a decent manner, then you have to be polite. If you want your child to respect everyone, then you have to respect them first.

If you want children to know that lying is a bad habit, then you should also not lie to them. If you want your child to be disciplined, then first, you have to be disciplined yourself. Whatever your personality and thinking is, the child will most probably follow suit.

If you want that your child should be good in academics, then have an environment of studying in the house and you should also show interest in studies.

It should never happen that you restrict access to the T.V. and the computer for the children but always be in front of them yourself.

Do not use foul languages around the house as children, being great imitators, learn them immediately.

At home, speak politely with the servants, if there are any.

Don't follow activities in front of the child which you are denying to him.

Try not to bring negative energy into your house. The child gets easily affected by the atmosphere in the house. Fighting in the house affects the child badly. Parents should not quarrel before the children. If they have any dispute, they should try to resolve it in private, not in the presence of the child. If the husband doesn't respect his wife, or vice versa, the children will also do that. Children will inculcate good values only from a suitably good home environment. In a joint family, your child will observe the way you treat your parents or elders and treat you accordingly. A person who misbehaves with his old father will most probably get the same behaviour from his child in the future.

So don't give only advice but set an example. Be a role model for the child.

The children are precious creation of the world.

They are our bright future.

Make the children cheerful

Children who are cheerful, good natured and amusing often are well liked by everyone. Cheerful nature starts at an early age. Hence cheer them up so that they can be healthy and cheerful.

A cheerful and jolly nature person makes the serious and dull atmosphere lighten up by his jolly nature and faces even the most difficult situation in future with a smile.

Jolly nature does not means that the child makes fun of others.

If we have taught the child to have a joyful nature even in adverse conditions then, it will help him in the future.

To make a child jolly, it is necessary that you behave friendly with him and share jokes with him.

It is also necessary to give ample chance for the development of imagination power of the child. To say common things in an uncommon way by use of imagination makes the listener happy.

In the same way, the jolly nature of a child can be enhanced by interesting stories, poems and jokes etc.

Beating affects the child adversely

Parents punish children in different ways when they make a mistake, by scolding them, by warning them and by beating them.

Often parents forget that whether they are beating the child in private or in front of someone. When the child is beaten before someone, he feels humiliated. In this condition, either he tries to retaliate or becomes dull and submissive. Both these conditions are bad for the child.

Keep your anger in control. Never throw things down or shout when you are angry. Parents are role models for their child. They observe all of the parents' activities minutely. Many times beating produces a result that we regret afterwards.

Repeated beating makes the child hide from parents and he starts lying to conceal his mistakes.

In hid adolescence, the child becomes rebellious. He answers back rudely, doesn't pay attention to their advice and becomes very wilful. This is the time when beating will not affect him. The parents realise that they have lost hold over the child and can only regret their past actions.

Making noise, shouting, jumping is generally not misbehaviour on the part of the child. These are often his way of growing up and developing. If a child actually misbehaves, then instead of beating him, make him understand that what type of behaviour is acceptable and what is not. Many times diverting the mind of a child also changes his behaviour. If you have to punish then it can be done by cancelling his movie or picnic etc.

Understanding their requirements and necessities, advise them gently. If you simply punish them instead of talking with them then, they will lose their self confidence. Low confidence leads to inferiority complex which is bad for his future.

Maintain the self respect of children

We generally make the mistake that self respect is only for adults. This is absolutely wrong. A child is much more sensitive than an adult. Fatal effects of ignoring self respect of children are seen when they get inferiority complex and become introverted.

When the parents criticize the children before other people or tease them unnecessarily, then trust and respect for the parents decreases in the children. The children feel the lack of intimacy. Then, family matters and affairs do not bother them and as a result, in the future, parents complain of their neglect by their children.

Punishing the child in front of others or criticising him before his friends affects the mind of the child a lot to.

Never compare two children. Each child has his own personality and attributes.

He will think ill of and dislike the one he is being compared to. The child will think that of the he is being compared to as his rival. Instead of comparison, it is better to nourish the child by giving due respect for his own unique talents.

Discriminating between a male and female child also hurts the self respect of the child. Give same respect, love, affection and importance to both.

We never pay attention to our faults and mistakes but rebuke or beat the child for trifle things. This adversely affects the self respect of the child very much. As a result the child might adopt reactionary and rebellious behaviour. When a child is frequently scolded by parents, he will feel like not staying at home.

Sometimes if a child wants to do something, the parents not only interrupt but also scold them. The child becomes mortified. He also feels insulted at that time. So explain properly to the child the reasons for you not letting him do what he wants.

If we want that our child to be like us and for them to have behaviour acceptable to us, then it is necessary that we must not hurt their self respect.

> **The greatest happiness in the life of children is that someone loves them unconditionally.**

Prevent deviation

To care for the child does not only mean loving them and understanding their requirements but also being vigilant about all their activities and preventing any deviant behavioural traits.

During childhood, pay attention to the habits of the child like abusing, fighting with elders, quarrelling, stealing etc. Don't ignore the bad habits of the child. Make him understand properly by telling him any example or story. Give love to the child in every situation but don't encourage him when he makes mistakes. Tell him that you love him very much, but you don't like his bad habits and punishment might be necessary if he does not comply.

First of all, change your own habits if you are also having such habits, because a child gets these habits from his family members. These bad habits can be removed at the beginning as children are easier to mould and change. If the child's bad habits are not discouraged, it'll become difficult in the future, as he becomes habituated to it.

A child is like clay, which can be moulded in any way by the potter but once it is fashioned, its shape cannot be amended later.

If you give sufficient pocket money to the child then you must keep a note of how he is spending it.

Nowadays joint family systems are disappearing. So when the child passes through mental and physical changes, often he finds himself alone without anyone to guide him. He can get into bad company easily as he needs someone to talk to.

Parents must spend ample time with their children in this situation. The more time they spend with them, the better the children will mix with them and can share their feeling with parents without any hesitation.

Why do children run away (abscond) from home?

A child generally feels ignored, unsafe and alone in those families where the atmosphere of dispute remains. He feels that his presence is worthless and his ability is neglected.

Generally parents think that absolute strict control is necessary towards their children. With this attitude, children are interrupted again and again and always given too much advice and instruction. For the sake of discipline, some parents start scolding/beating the child before their friends.

Such type of behaviour makes the child introverted; his self respect gets hurt.

Within the family, difference and discrimination in the treatment of the children, like considering one child superior to the other also becomes the cause for the tendency of the child to abscond from home. If one child gets excess love, then the other child might feel ignored.

The child never takes the decision of leaving running away from home suddenly. Before he does it, he thinks about it for a long time. When the unsafe, ignorant and choking atmosphere becomes unbearable to him, only then he thinks about running away from the home.

At that time, he doesn't think about the troubles he will face after leaving home.

The parents should understand that they should treat all their children equally and instead of the extremes of strict control or excess love and affection, adopt a balanced attitude towards the child.

Parents should take interest in the study, games and hobbies of their child and befriend him. Make him feel that he is not alone and that you are always with him in whatever situation he faces.

Befriend your children

Instead of keeping the child away from you or making him afraid, it will be better to befriend him. Sit with him when he returns from school. Ask him about his day in school. Take the child out with you to social events as much as possible. He will be introduced to the outer world and gets ready to face the outer world fearlessly. After befriending your child, you can solve many of his problems easily. For example, you can immediately recognize when he is in a sad mood or disappointed or being quiet and you can ask the reason. As the child gets used to you, he will immediately tell you everything.

A child often passes through many situations like, not being able to adjust with the school atmosphere or problems in understanding any chapter in class. So spare some time and try to listen to him. If you listen to the child calmly, then you can win his trust and confidence. Don't ignore him by considering his matter as childish, as his emotions are as important as of an adult person and he is depending on you.

A child will be eager to tell you all his activities if he is used to telling you from childhood. So build such relations with the child from the beginning so that there is no hesitation while sharing feelings and stories.

Every child wants sincere appreciation for his good work. He wants to get appreciation from his parents and siblings. He starts doing good work when he gets the appropriate response. We should try to know his mentality by thinking at his level. If the base of a friendly nature is built in him, then everything becomes easy. Parents are required to try and nourish the child as a combined effort. Enhance positive attitude in the child.

For family entertainment, from time to time, plan to go for picnic, sightseeing, sailing or short tours. At the time of planning take the opinions of the children into consideration. The more the parents talk to the children, the more frank the children will become with them. They will feel safe with their parents.

Parents should be friendly with them and only then the child can trust them. Consider their opinion important so that they can give it freely. They must think of the parents as important to their progress, thoughts, friendships and development. Unanimity between the old and new generations is the success of friendship.

By becoming children with children, parents can influence and teach their children as much as they can't by becoming elder.

Don't hover around
The child all the time

Do you think that the child is irritated or trying to ignore you even if you are behaving like a friend on every matter from study to games? There is no mistake of the child here. It is a mistake on your part that you hover around him always. You might be showing excessive interest in all his activities like school projects, selection of friends, extracurricular activities or even in simple harmless fun.

When you keep the child under your vigil all the time, then, the child thinks that you don't trust him. Keep an eye on him just to reassure him that he is in a safe zone. Be his friend but up to a limit. Hovering around always or not letting him take any decision can make him rebellious or dull.

Teach your child the right values

Many people use young children as thieves and also, especially in big/joint families, children are often used to spy on the activities of other family members. These kinds of activities lead to deterioration in morals as well as have adverse psychological effects on the children involved. If such a child grows up to have warped moral or ethical values, it should not come as a surprise.

Never get children involved in any sort of adult disputes involving family members. If there is any problem with other family members and in laws, do not drag the child into the mess.

If there is a quarrel between parents or other family members, and neither wants to communicate directly with the other, do not make the child a messenger to carry messages to each other. The child does not need to hear about your personal views or disputes with one another and such a situation will only make the child more insecure and bewildered.

Often it is seen that many women cannot do certain things in the presence of their husbands. Perhaps they fear his disapproval and prefer to do it when the husbands are away. However in secrecy, they do often do such things in front of their child and warn the child not to tell the father. This type of clandestine behaviour is not to be done as it also affects the child's psyche adversely.

Parents may sometimes not agree and quarrel over issues relating to the raising of the child. The father might say something to the child but the mother might deny it or vice-versa. Do not put the child in such difficult situation. This sort of contradictory instructions puzzles the child and it is not good for his discipline. Parents should as much as possible agree on what to say to the child. Parents should try to have similar mind sets as much as possible regarding their children.

Often, it is seen that parents talk negatively about other family members and relatives before the child. You should avoid this kind of behaviour as such a negative environment is not good for the child's development.

If the child steals things

A child, who has an inferiority complex or doesn't have a stable personality, sometimes adopts the habit of stealing. Many a times, a child may bring something back from school that he has stolen and claim that he found it somewhere. In this situation, it is necessary to keep a vigil on the child. But be careful to first ascertain the validity of his story and make sure that he doesn't realize that he is under watch.

The child's bag must be checked regularly.

If you find any new items in his possession, that you had no knowledge of, then ask him first about where or from whom he got it. If the child is clearly lying, prod gently and firmly but do not be harsh or angry.

Do not punish or scold the child immediately when he steals something. The knee-jerk reaction of punishment will not make the habit go away. Always criticize the stealing habit but not the child personally. Make the child understand his mistake in such a way that he will not lash out or refuse to say anything more. Gently but firmly tell him that he must return what he stole and that there is no shame in returning it as everyone makes mistakes but he should not repeat it again.

In the meantime, you must try to ascertain what the reason behind his habit of stealing is. Is it simply greed or lack of pocket money or pressure from peers or for sheer amusement, etc? Observe the situation carefully and without any bias.

Parents must remember that, an incident of stealing if it happens once, if handled properly with patience and care, can become a good opportunity to teach him a life lesson that he will never forget.

If the child steals things

Teach him properly the difference between right and wrong. Give him such strong moral values that in any situation, he will not be tempted to take what does not belong to him steal. Make him understand that he will not give in even when pressured by friends or peers to do so. In this kind of a situation, parents' contribution is to give proper guide and a lot of love and attention to the child.

Teaching children the value of money

Spending within limit is an important moral and practical value. Not only money but all other resources should also be spent wisely and in the right way.

Low income group families are recommended to save about 1/3rd or 1/4th part of their incomes for emergencies or for the children's further studies or for the marriage of their children in the future.

Even those who are wealthy should not be too extravagant. This habit of extravagance will be imitated by your children and this will pose a problem as they grow up. They might be unable to cope if there is sudden loss of the wealth due to unfortunate circumstances.

If you spend on unnecessary things, then you might not have the resources to spare for religious matters or public welfare, and your child might follow your trend which is not healthy for his over all development.

Often low income families have to suffer the most due to the lack of resources and the house is often is chaos.

Since it is more common for women to stay home and look after the children and the house, a lot depends on them relating to teaching the children how to save and spend money as well as managing the income of the family

Teaching children how to accept defeat gracefully

It is important to teach children not only to win but also to accept defeat gracefully. In life, one cannot win all the time and so, it is important to teach this lesson to your child so that he does not get disheartened or discouraged when he does not win and he can pick himself up and move forward when he falls down.

To feel disheartened after a defeat is common but teach the child to bear that defeat gracefully. You can help him in analyzing where he might have gone wrong and suggest ways for improvement. Encourage him by saying things like "if you try again by working on your weak points, then you will surely win."

Many times it is seen that parents are very harsh on the child when he faces defeat regularly. However, any parent should know that, this is the time when he needs your emotional support the most. One sincere encouraging pat from you can pull him out of the agony and humiliation of defeat.

Encourage the child to always give his best in everything. Tell him that participating whole heartedly is always more important than winning.

When a child faces failure, parents should tell him that it is not the end of his ability but the beginning of new avenues. As one door closes, other doors will open automatically. Encourage the child and remind him that he has all the ability and talent required for success and success will surely be his one day.

Discouraging superstitions (blind faith) in children

Our society is rife with superstition and this has been ingrained in us for so long that we are often guilty of accepting and promoting blind superstitions without really using our judgment to see if they hold some truth or not.

Our modern society is often guilty of following many superstitions for the sake of rituals and traditions which may have lost meaning but we continue to follow because we have been doing so for the past generations.

To introduce and ingrain superstitions in the child's mind is not being wise but being foolish as he might remain ingrained in them throughout his life.

At least for the sake of the health of the newly born baby, take all decisions based on a qualified doctor's advice and do not be dependent on superstitious beliefs.

Discipline

A disciplined child will be a good citizen and a productive member of society. It is needed to teach discipline in a proper way without hindering the progress of the development of the child and all his unique abilities. In order to teach children discipline, parents have to make a time table for themselves first. If the parents are self disciplined, then children will also generally follow suit. Don't make it a habit of making the child do his work by tempting him with treats or by threatening him with punishments. Also if you have promised something to your child, then you must fulfil it. To show inconsistency in your attitude towards a specific work is not right. For example, do not praise the child sometimes and scold him at other times for the same work.

If the parents give excessive freedom to the child in the beginning and later on, impose too many restrictions, then the child might start to become rebellious and he might go down the wrong path just to spite the parents. It is better to give such freedom to the children for which they are mentally prepared. Excessive freedom might also spoil the child and make him wilful and this can create problems for the parents.

Try to make your opinion clear to the child in the right way so that he doesn't question or doubt your decision. If necessary, the reason can be explained logically so that the child will accept your opinion with respect and not with fear.

Discipline means to make the child self controlled by showing some practical examples. Discipline cannot be taught by beatings or scoldings.

We can be disciplined when we make rules and follow them.

For example

1. Everyone must always treat each other with respect.
2. Everyone must take full responsibility for their own actions.
3. Nobody should leave the house without permission or without telling anyone.
4. Must not watch T.V without finishing home work.

Discipline should be helpful for children and not distressful.

Disciplining should be consistent. Punishment for a mistake one time, while ignoring the same mistake another time, is not effective.

If the child makes a mistake then don't beat him but try to find out the reason behind it and find a proper solution for that.

Award the child when he does something good and if he does something wrong, punish him after explaining why it is wrong.

If the child is refusing to do some work then, you must ask the reason for that.

If the child refuses go to school/college, then it will not be good to punish him blindly without knowing the reason behind his reluctance.

If the child is insisting on something, then you must know why he is insisting. Get to know the company he keeps and guide him properly.

Parents should keep a control on themselves before they try to control the children. If you are not disciplined at home then how can you teach your offspring?

Disciplining should help the children and not frustrate them.

Encourage the child

Whenever your child does commendable work like doing well academically or performs well in games or any other work in societal gatherings, then, praise and reward him and encourage him. Encouragement has the power to push one to do better.

Encourage the children to ask questions so that their curiosity may be satisfied and their knowledge about many things will increase.

Give them a chance to put forward their point of view. They must feel that their opinion is considered valuable.

When the child helps you or other people, then praise him and show physical affection. This encourages him to be helpful and do good deeds.

It is very important to praise the child for his good work and encourage him for that.

> **By encouraging the children, those power can be developed on which his health success and happiness depend.**

Formation of character

Strong character or morality in a man provides him courage when he faces problems. Character formation and education of moral values should start early in a child.

Simply giving righteous advices and moral instructions have no affect till they are accompanied by action.

Children have the tendency to imitate and they make idols of their parents or nearest ones, hanging on to their every word and gesture. On the basis of all that, a child's character is developed.

If the child lives in an environment of constant criticism, he learns to condemn everything.

If the child lives in an environment of praise, then he learns to appreciate.

If the child lives in an environment of hostility, then he learns to be defensive and aggressive.

If the child lives in an environment of tolerance, then he learns to be patient.

If the child lives in an environment of ridicule, then he will become shy and introverted.

If the child lives in an environment of encouragement, then he learns to be confident.

If the child lives in an environment of shame, then he learns to always feel guilty even where doesn't need to feel so.

If the child lives in an environment of approval, then he learns to like and appreciate himself and his abilities.

If the child lives in an environment of fairness, then he learns to be just.

Formation of character

If the child lives in an environment of security, then he learns to feel secure and trust people.

If the child lives in an environment of acceptance and friendship, then he learns to find love in the world.

As the thoughts, so will be the character.

Enhance self confidence in children

Self confidence is the key to success. Parents have the main role in enhancing self confidence in children. The environment in the house, family and surroundings affect the level of self confidence in the children. If the parents are capable, then the children will be full of self confidence.

Adopt a liberal attitude
Children, like all human beings, make mistakes but they should never be beaten or scolded.

But try to get them to learn something from their mistake. They must be encouraged to rectify their mistakes and acquire new ideas in their mind. They must be taught how to face challenges and how to tackle the problem if the same situation happens again a second time.

If the parents show the child the right path whenever he makes a mistake, then he can rectify his mistakes easily.

Understanding the thoughts of the children

Generally the parents ignore the talks and thoughts of their child. However this is wrong. Parents should pay heed to how their child thinks on a particular topic and what is the direction of his intention. By doing so, you can help him in recognising the right facts and help make his attitude positive. Whenever the child talks to you, listen to him carefully and try to understand his ideas. It will increase his self confidence.

Enhance the self confidence
School students should be given a chance to do their work themselves. This enhances self-confidence in the child and he does not get confused when he faces difficult challenges.

Don't make unnecessary comparisons

Stay away from unnecessarily comparing children to one another. It affects the mentality of children adversely and they lose faith in their capability and ability.

Keep on appreciating

Always appreciate all the work (even small ones) completed by the child and praise his hard work. This makes the child happy and he tries to do much better in the future. Contrary to this, if you try to find mistakes in their work all the time, then they get distressed.

Encourage

Encourage the power, work efficiency and capability of the child and if possible try to help change his weaknesses into his strength.

> **Don't tell children how to do things. Tell them what to do and let them find their own way of doing it.**

Build a strong base of ethics in children

Ethics play an important role in the overall development of the child. Strong ethics form a base for development of good character and personality.

Teach your children to respect their elders. To respect elders is one of the most important moral values. This is only possible when you yourself respect your elders. Also, do tell your child the importance of loving their younger siblings and caring for them. Encourage the child from time to time.

Tell your child that he will be lovable to everyone if he loves his younger brother or sister and cares for them. Teach him that respect and love is gotten only when we give love and respect to others.

Most of the time, the mother is the teacher for her child from the time of birth till he joins a school or preschool. Though children are mentally or physically delicate when they're very young, but still they are curious. Children want to know about everything around them. Give them suitable answers and satisfy their curiosity as much as you can.

Teach them about the importance of cleanliness, sanitation, courtesy, virtuous behaviour, truthfulness, honesty, hard work, right moral values, self reliance, discipline etc. with proper examples from the time of childhood itself. With the help of legends and stories you can introduce them to the history of the country, community and religion, culture, etc. Tell them about the life stories of great personalities, other talented children, heroes who sacrificed their lives for the country, virtuous women as well as about festivals like Bhaiya Dooj and Raksha Bandhan etc.

Build a strong base of ethics in children

Children also learn many things from reading books. It is the duty of parents to get them suitable books by reading which they can learn good values and develop and achieve their goals.

Teach our precious traditional culture and accomplishments to the children, so that younger generations may not be deprived of them. Any education is not complete till the child learns to respect his country. Tell the child that the country is like the home that he lives in.

As said before, children get a lot of their knowledge from the behaviour of their parents and are very affected by them. So by adopting good behaviour, manner and thoughts and by giving adequate means of development, we can make the child virtuous.

Emotional development of children

The emotional development of the children also plays a big role in their mental and physical development. Generally the child who is emotionally strong will healthy, bright and socially adaptable.

For emotional development

1. Hug your child at least once a day as it will improve emotional relations between you.

2. Every child should have the assurance in his mind that his parents love him.

3. Every child should have a secure feeling in his heart that he is a safe member of the home, family and society that he belongs to.

4. We should respect the independent thoughts, imagination and opinion of the child.

5. It is necessary to help the child and solve his problems during his adverse situations and uncertainty.

6. Let the child play with other children so that he can develop his nature in accordance with others of his age.

7. Discipline is must for the children, but parents should not be overly harsh in implementing it.

8. Occasionally, encourage the child by praising him or giving him rewards.

9. The child must get proper guidance under the protection and affection of his parents.

10. The child should have the feeling that his parents have faith in him and wants him to succeed. For this, the child should get complete freedom for his work and undertakings.

11. The child should have the firm faith that even after making a mistake, his parents will still love him and if they punish him, it is for his own welfare.

12. Tell the children about the importance of the simple works of charity from the beginning.

13. Show children the wonder of nature and teach them to appreciate it.

14. Teach the elder child that the responsibility for his younger sibling(s) lies on him.

15. Teach the younger child also to respect his elder sibling(s).

Don't ignore the curiosity of the children. All their sensible and insensible questions must be answered in brief by discussion, so that they get satisfied and don't think that they are being disregarded

Social and spiritual development of the children

Social and spiritual development plays a main role for the bright future of children.

For social and spiritual development

1. Teach the child to bow and show respectful gestures.

2. Teach the child to be polite and teach them to use polite words like sorry, please, thank you, excuse me, etc. at the appropriate times.

3. When you are at any religious places, tell them to be quiet and bow respectfully by touching both hands. Tell them to respect all religions and do not criticize any religion in front of them.

4. Teach them to treat everyone as equal, whether he is a servant working in your house, a member of the school staff or a shopkeeper, etc. The child should know that a man should be given respect not due to his status or wealth but due to the fact that he is a human being.

5. Encourage the children to take part in religious and spiritual activities. It should never be thought by them that praying and worshiping is only for adults. A simple way to keep the child attached to tradition and culture is an adherence to the religious functions and activities. Praying every morning makes the child confident and gives him good thoughts.

Social and spiritual development of the children

6. To help a child to be socially well adjusted and adaptable, give proper chances to the children to mix with others at the time of festivals, etc. and also celebrate their birthdays with enthusiasm, inviting their friends and other people over.

7. Never tolerate crude words from the mouth of children even if they have said them in jest.

8. Give proper instructions also, that before using anyone else's things, they must take permission from the person concerned even if they are very close to each other.

9. Tell the children that not everyone is fortunate to always eat good food and so they must not waste food or be fussy about it.

10. They must be clearly taught that garbage must be thrown in dustbin and not strewn around anywhere.

Realisation of responsibility

Inculcate the habit of making the child do his routine work himself.

Whatever habit you want to teach children, it should be done properly and in a systematic manner so that they don't think of it like a burden. If they have to be responsible in the future, then why should they not start early, even if it is done casually?

Encourage them to do their own personal work and assign house work according to their age. Examples—

1. To keep their toys back in their proper places.

2. To empty the water bottle and school bag after coming back from school.

3. To keep their shoes in their proper places. To arrange and put personal things like school uniform, belt, handkerchief, socks, tie and shoes etc. back in their proper places at night.

4. Fill empty bottles and put in the fridge.

5. To arrange the dining table at dinner time, put utensils back in kitchen after meals and cleaning the table, etc.

6. To help out the mother in cleaning the house and arranging the bookshelf etc.

7. To keep the dirty clothes in the laundry basket.

8. Older children can help their mother in the kitchen by cutting fruits and salad if they can handle a knife.

9. Let the child know properly as to where the pulses and spices are kept.

10. Teach them to sew buttons that might have fallen off.

11. Running errands like, to get things from the nearby market. It will also them develop their estimation of quality when they shop in the future.

12. To help the mother in other small works in the kitchen.

13. To respect guests and treat them well in the presence or absence of the parents.

14. To answer telephone calls politely and to take note of the messages, if any.

Note –
1. Don't assign any task to him, which you yourself don't want to do, i.e. do not make the child your servant.
Make him do work so that he can understand his responsibilities.
2. If necessary, parents must co-operate with their children. For example, some parents themselves complete the project of their children and send them to school. Co-operate with them only in helping them make the project but don't make it yourself. This way the child, as a student, will become self confident.

Make the child face every situation so that he can learn to face the challenge in difficult and disastrous situation.

Enhance creative thinking in children

To think creatively means to think of new ideas, new innovations and new solutions. Creative thinking makes the mind sharp and there is less mental tension.

Different ways of enhancing creative thinking

1. Sit with the child and put in front of him anything that is used daily and everyone present should say one by one, various uses of that thing. You can make it like a game.
2. Similarly, present a problem suitable to the age of the child and tell him to try and find its solution.
3. Family members along with the children should have gatherings in which exchange of ideas on different topics may take place.
4. You can also have puzzle solving sessions.
5. You can discuss about the many different ways of doing one work.

Every human of this world has a specific quality of his highlighted for which the world is waiting.

Your children and their friends

As children grow into adolescence, their connections with their friends increase exponentially.

Generally an adolescent prefers to talk to friends and starts turning away from parents. The more he sees the outer world, the more he strays from the home. To be scolded on every matter is disliked by the child of this age and the result may be that the distance between parents and child increases.

For a good relationship to develop, it is very necessary to talk to each other. Know about his interest and his friends and talk about them. Call his friends home and sit with them. Befriend your child but don't try to take the place of his friend.

To bring the child nearer to you, you should share your happy and sad moments with him. This also gives him a chance to learn. At a growing age, children are very close to their friends, but they also need parents' support.

As he grows up, a child will meet many people. You should teach him how to distinguish between people who are good and those who are bad for him. Tell them how the meaning of relations and friendships change as they grow older. To make good relations with someone he has to work hard. You must tell your children that many relations may be there only up to a certain age. Not all relations formed last a whole lifetime.

If you think that your child has fallen into bad company, do not be hasty in your actions. The child can be brought back to the right path if you make him understand with love and patience. But if you get angry with him, the result may be the opposite. Instead, be slightly strict with him from beginning and keep an eye on all his friendships.

Keep a vigil on your child's friends

Try to know about the background of the parents of your child's friend and about his family atmosphere, because family environment affects the nature of the child. However this does not mean being judgmental

Observe your child (whether male or female) when he/she starts staying over at his/her friends house late. Enquire quietly from the parents of your child's friend as to the movements and timings of your child's visits.

Observe the behaviour of the child at home, and note if he speaks continuously or stops in between his narrations of the events of the day or tries to make excuses.

If the child is talking about a friend repeatedly then you must be observant about the new friendship. If he makes different excuses to go to his friend too many times, then you may be strict with him without hesitation.

Observe the friend with whom your child has formed a new close bond and note his mannerisms and way of talking. If you see anything undesirable in him, you must curb the new friendship, but subtly.

Note – If you get any complaints about your child, then don't scold him immediately but look at all the sides of the matter. Later, tell him what is right and what is wrong.

We should try so that the child never feels a lack of love from the parents and nor should he think that you are do not care about his feelings and opinions.

A child should always know that not everything will go according to his plan, and you, as a parent, are not clueless about his activities.

When children start asking awkward questions

Children often start asking awkward questions after watching the T.V. like—what is pregnancy? Or where do the babies come from? Or where do they come from? etc.

Parents often try to escape from such question. Don't get defensive with such questions and don't scold the child. It is in a child's nature to ask questions.

You must answer the question of the child with an answer suitable to his age, and up to the limit of his understanding.

Never give wrong information to the child. For example, when he asks where babies come from, do not answer that they come from the sky. Tell them that they come from the mother's belly.

Child molestation is on the rise now a days and so it is important to keep your child informed about people's good or bad intentions towards them. While bathing, you can tell your child, that if someone touches his private parts, then it is wrong.

Children can understand, so if someone teases them inappropriately they will tell you.

The conclusion is that if the children are to be taught about sex in a natural way, then it is always best to be open with them

Inform them about the physical changes of the body.

During adolescence, children get amazed with the changes in their body.

Parents can give the right information about the physical changes. You can also tell them that sexual abstinence is a good things and it will be better for their health and career.

Tell them to be careful of having relationships before marriage. Their emotional and physical health is always more important.

Studies reveal that children who can talk to their parents about sex are generally better informed about the pros and cons of sexual relationships during adolescence and after.

Sexual education

Most parents want have discussions on sexual education with their children but don't know how to start.

Adolescents need the love of parents. The father should talk frankly to the child about sex. This gives him proper knowledge about it. If they feel shy talking about sex, then you may send them to your family doctor.

The mother should give sexual education to her daughter Teenage girls are like buds which need to be nourished with extra care. Mothers' role plays a vital role in that.

The mother should give all the information about the physical changes that happens in the body of a girl according to the age. Being the mother, you can give the right information about menstrual periods, hygiene and sanitary napkins. In the same way during breast development, teach her to wear the right bra, clean the hair around sex organs and armpit etc.

When the girl grows older into adolescence, the mother should be careful, as this is the time when the mother can share her own experience related to sex with the daughter and give her proper direction. At this age, children are advised to be careful about relations with opposite sex, especially girls as often they are unaware about the resulting complications of pregnancy, abortion etc. To talk about this is considered the duty and responsibility of each mother.

If the child knows his limit of friendship, then the problem will not rise.

Making young girls into ideal women

Girls often take on the roles of being the daughter, daughter-in-law, wife and mother. Teach the girl child to take interest in household activities. Teach them from the beginning. Take their help in work associated traditionally with women, like sewing, embroidery, cooking, making special meals, caring for siblings, management of the house, cleaning, courtesy, home decoration etc. Along with school education, home education is also important for a girl and up to an extent, for a boy too.

Girls are generally believed to be more delicate, emotional and affectionate.

On the starting of adolescence, tell them how they to cope during menstruation periods. After marriage, generally, the responsibility of the husband and children will come to her. So it is necessary to develop decision making powers in your girl child.

Teach your child how to budget the income, and manage household, etc. Give her the proper knowledge of sex and about taking care of her health and safety. You can also advice her about the cleaning and care of the breasts and wearing the right bra size.

Teach your child to judge the intentions of a new person. Teach them how to behave with the different kinds of people they will meet, like colleagues, classmates, in laws, etc.

Keep an eye on your children's friends and their characters. You do not want your child to fall into bad company. At the same time, do not be overtly strict either as this may make them revolt.

A child's insistence on not going to school

This is a common problem parents face, that the child does not want to go to school or makes excuses not to or cries a lot.

One major reason behind this problem is that parents or someone in the house may be extra indulgent to the child and he may not want to leave the person even for few hours. In some other cases, the children may be weak in studies and, so they want to escape from the punishment of the teacher and humiliation in the school by fellow students.

There are some other reasons which make the child not want to go to school, like, he may not have done his home work or fears going on stage, is not ready on time, or thinks himself to be inferior to others.

What to do?

Don't admit the child in school at too young an age. If you want to send him to a play school then, send him to that kind of school where there is less study and more games in the curriculum.

The child should be encouraged before going to school. A little love and kind talk from your side can make the school sound like a comfortable place. Never say things about school which makes the child afraid of school.

Don't make the school out as a place of horror and instead present it as a better place.

Parents should create affection and liking towards the school in the child's heart and mind. Tell the child with love that by going to school he will come across many new things. He will get new friends and then he will become an accomplished person in life and for all that, going to school is necessary.

If a child still doesn't want to go to the school, then try to find out the reason behind that.

If a child returns from school in a bad mood, then ask gently that what the matter is. Ask if the teacher scolded him or he had a fight with his class mates. If the child complaints about a teacher or a class mate, then tell him that you will go to the school and talk to them. You should go to school and ask about it but never accuse the teacher. This may increase the distance between the teacher and child. Never criticize the teacher in front of child but always tell him to respect the teacher.

> **To eliminate out the doubt and fear from the child, ensure him directly or indirectly that you are with him to remove any problems and doubts.**

Sending the child to school is not the end of your duties

School is the important place for natural development. The first outer world for the child is school.

Parents' involvement can boost a child's interest in studies. Those children comparatively do better in studies, whose parents check their diary and home work daily and keep a track on their progress.

When the child returns from school, it is the responsibility of the mother or father to ask about his day.

It should always be kept in mind that school is not the only place from where children learn something. A child learns in every step he takes and attains accomplishments.

It is obvious that the effect of home, family and environment of the surroundings influence a child much more than school.

So do not think that sending the child to school is the only duty you have, but also remember your responsibility for his overall development.

The main contribution to their training is not by giving instruction or advice but by setting examples. The child has infinite power. They are enthusiastic all the time. To focus that enthusiasm in the right direction is the key to make them better human beings and this is possible by becoming role models for the kids and not just giving advices.

Ability and the interest of the child should be encouraged in the right direction. They should not be given negative instructions like 'don't do this, don't do that' 'should never be spoken' but instead we can say 'do this, do that' etc.

They should not be given unnecessary indulgences or scolded unnecessarily. They should not be allowed to be undisciplined nor overly submissive. Don't spoil them to such an extent that they cannot bear little extra heat and cold.

The curiosity of the child's mind should not be ignored. They have new questions every moment. The answers to their questions should be given in a simple and intelligent way. They should not be scolded or deferred. A child gets full mental development when his/her questions are answered.

> **The aim of education is not to compel the child to read or write but to co-operate in all his works to develop his various capabilities.**

Create on ideal atmosphere for the child while studying

To maintain the interest of a child in academics, the ideal atmosphere is necessary. For study, first of all train the children to concentrate.

Their study room should be calm and quiet. There should be no T.V. in the study room.

The study of the child should not get disturbed on the arrival of a guest.

During the study time, there should not be any activity around, which interrupts the child again and again. Teach the student that whatever he has learned; repeat all that in his/her mind by closing the eyes. Then, write that in the note book once. Those children who are in the vicinity of fumes of smoking often have lower rate of brain development, so keep them away from smoking.

Along with study, health care is also important.

Exercise and fresh air is also necessary for a creative brain.

Gyan mudra and meditation enhances the memory power.

Letter of a father to the son's teacher

(Written by American President Abraham Lincoln)

He will have to learn, I know, that all men are not just, all men are not true, but teach him also that for every scoundrel there is a hero; that for every selfish politician, there is a dedicated leader, teach him for every enemy there is a friend. Steer him away from envy. If you can, teach him the secret of quiet laughter.

Let him learn early that the bullies are the easiest to lick. Teach him, if you can, the wonder of books, but also give him quiet time to ponder the eternal mystery of birds in the sky, bees in the sun, and the flowers on a green hillside.

In the school teach him it is far honourable to fail than to cheat. Teach him to have faith in his own ideas, even if everyone tells him they are wrong. Teach him to be gentle with gentle people, and tough with the tough.

Try to give my son the strength not to follow the crowd when everyone is getting on the band wagon. Teach him to listen to all men, but teach him also to filter all he hears on a screen of truth, and take only the good that comes through.

Teach him if you can, how to laugh when he is sad. Teach him there is no shame in tears. Teach him to scoff at cynics and to beware of too much sweetness. Teach him to sell his brawn and brain to the highest bidders but never to put a price-tag on his heart and soul.

Teach him to close his ears to a howling mob and to stand and fight if he thinks he's right. Treat him gently, but do not cuddle him, because only the test of fire makes fine steel.

Let him have the courage to be impatient, let him have the patience to be brave. Teach him always to have sublime faith in himself, because then he will have sublime faith in mankind.

This is a big order but see what you can do. He is such a fine little fellow, my son!

Tuition for the children

In the era of competition, all parents want that their child to be ahead always. So children are sent for tuitions from the beginning. In this situation if they have to go for tuition after school, they cannot get proper relaxation and it affects their study. Academics will seem as a burden to them and their curiosity it will end.

Let the child rest after coming back from school. Then, give him something to eat and after that you ask about school and his study. Check his school notebook and copies. If the child has done well, then you must appreciate it.

If the child has left incomplete work in school then, don't scold him. It will be better if you ask the reason for that. Teach the child not seriously, but a little casually, making it like a game and he will start taking interest. Help him cultivate a good handwriting and appreciate him on writing well and doing good work. This encourages the self confidence of the child and also his faith on you.

Send him for tuitions when it is unavoidable. For example, when the mental development of the child is not according to his age or both parents are illiterate or semi-illiterate, or there is a language problem or he is weak in a particular subject. However parents should not be careless after sending the child for tuition. Search for a good tutor and tell him about your expectations from him. Always ask the child about the tuition sessions and if there is any problem, be in contact with the tutor.

During the examination time of children

Thinking or hearing of impending examinations, children often lose their appetite due to stress. They cannot sleep and become anxious. These things are common. So, during the exam time, both child and parents should try to be free from tension.

Don't let them study the whole night. If they remain awake the whole night, they will not be able to remember what they have studied and because they should get proper sleep.

Don't give them heavy meals during examinations as the body needs extra energy to digest this type of meal and nerve energy, required for studying decreases.

During examinations, give light and digestible food like salads in plenty. It keeps drowsiness away and he can concentrate on his study.

Do not scold the child during examination time. Make him understand by talking and discussing with him.

Don't ban all games and other activities during examinations as the child needs to relax during exams too.

Parents ambition (dream) – burden on the child

Parents often expect too much from their children without knowing their capability or interest.

Don't expect the child to deliver more than his capacity. In a class, it is not possible that all students can come first. If the child does not stand first, he should not be punished physically or mentally.

When the child does a little better then, it will be good for the parents to show that they are proud of him, instead of pressing him to do better. Motivate him to try further but do not press him to bring much better marks.

In many families generally it is seen that if one of the children is better in academics, in comparison to the other, who might be average, then the parents favour the former more. This discrimination may hurt the latter child. Parents must know that every child is unique.

Do not always appreciate the child who is doing better. Unknowingly, the other child will get an inferiority complex.

All children should not be judged with the same eye and they cannot be dealt with the same tactics. Parents should not press the child to push beyond their limits.

A child should be compared with his own previous performance and not with another person.

It is more important for parents to try and make their child a good human being rather than just a good scholar.

When the child fails in examinations

When a child fails in an examination, then he needs support from his family, not their scolding.

If a child fails in an examination, then it becomes your moral duty as a parent to support him so that he can prepare himself for that situation. If at that time he does not get your support then, it might take a wrong step or suffer from an inferiority complex forever.

In reality, the child is more distressed as compared to your distress on his failure, because ultimately it is happening to him, not you.

Tell him to analyze the reason for his failure, instead of being hopeless and desperate, so that the cause can be rectified next time.

A child gets shocked mentally when he fails. So, at this time he needs your affectionate touch, sensitive advice and mature behaviour.

Tell your child that failure is the pillar for success.

Don't scold the child and don't taunt him by giving examples of any other child, as all children are not alike.

Encourage the child who has met failure so that he can start again with full and renewed energy.

Recognize the child's talent

Do you think that your child is a genius? If not, then try to look inside him. Maybe that he has a lot of capabilities which are being ignored.

All children have a hidden talent or more. Many talented children cannot show their talent by the yard stick of academics alone.

Only pen and paper test cannot judge the entire talents of a child. While one child might have the surprising ability to create things, another one might have a strong imagination power and someone might have the capability of leadership. These things often cannot be measured by school activities alone. Examples are —

1. Some children can make the Eiffel Tower or other things with common things lying around at home. These characteristics in young children are the indications that they have the talent to be architectural designers.

2. Some children from a young age learn to save their pocket money for important things. This indicates that they have the ability to be good at business.

3. Some children are good at arranging and managing things. These are the strong indications of leadership and organisational capability.

4. Some children are curious to know about everything around them. If the talent of such children are supported and nourished then, they can be scientists or journalists.

5. Some children can gradually and casually create stories, and their imagination power is miraculous. Encourage such children, one day they can become good writers.

Recognize the child's talent

6. Some children talk a lot. To gossip in the class is their habit. You cannot stop them from talking but make sure that it is not malicious or harmful. Such children often have the ability to be good lawyers or can be successful in media.

In the other similar ways, indications of different talents can be looked for in children.

Note – A single child can have many talents he can perform well in more than one field simultaneously.

Generally parents do not take such extracurricular talents seriously and a child has to follow conventional careers that their parents espouse. This affects the performance of the child directly, which may prove to be their undoing a lot.

Most parents know about the older, conventional careers and so they want the child to move on those tried and tested paths. Today, however, there are many more different options of careers but they might not have information about that.

Sometimes the parents pressure the child to choose the career that their relatives and friends have chosen. There are more than 3000 careers in the competitive world today and we should not remain closed to any of them.

Often, the result which one gets from the non-traditional, new track of careers is amazing.

According to experts, parents and teachers should look in the direction in which the child is taking interest. Then encourage the child in the same direction and help him. This will improve his performance in that field and he will be self confident because any one will do better in that field in which he has interest.

In choosing the career of a child, choice cannot be given without proper knowledge on the part of the parents. To instruct them properly is also necessary.

In the parents' social circle, there may be many friends who have different careers. Introduce your child to them. It is a fact that sometimes the child chooses wrong career by just looking at what his peers are doing. If the child wants really to do something different then, listen to his arguments.

Higher studies with the help of education loans

For the middle class, often, it is troublesome to get the funds for the higher education of their children, but this dream can be fulfilled by education loan.

Who can take such loans?

1. He should be an Indian citizen.
2. The age should be between 16-26 years.
3. Get excellent marks in exams.
4. Parents should have a stable source of income.
5. He has applied for a regular course of any University in India or abroad or has been selected for that.

Procedure and necessary documents for a loan

1. Fill the application form for the education loan. You can fill it at any near commercial bank or you can fill it online.
2. All the relevant certificates and marks sheet related to the level of education.
3. Authority letter of the college in which you are taking admission.
4. Identity proof, residence proof and age certificate.
5. You should have a valid visa and passport if you are going to take admission abroad.
6. Income proof of parents.

Expenditure usually covered by education loans

1. Tuition fees.
2. Examination, library and lab fees.
3. Expenditure for books and equipments needed.
4. If you are going abroad for study then, travelling expenses are included.
5. Expenditure incurred on study tours, project works and on thesis.
6. Expenditure on the purchase of a computer or laptop etc.

Loan amount

1. If you are taking a loan to study within the country, then you can get a loan of up to ten lakhs.
2. If you are taking a loan to study abroad, you can get a loan up to 20 lakhs.
3. The rate of interest for every bank may be different. Still, it usually remains between 11 to 13%.
4. If you are taking a loan of about 4 lakhs then, there is no need for any security but if the loan amount is more than 4 lakhs then you need a security or surety.

Loan repayment

After the completion of the course or after getting a job (whichever is earlier) you have to start paying the instalments towards paying back the loan.

Rebate on Tax

If you have taken an educational loan, you can claim income tax deduction under Section 80-E.

1. On an education loan, only the individual will get rebate, not the HUF or any other.

2. The amount you are paying as interest will be considered as deduction. You will not get any deduction on the principal amount.

3. There is no upper limit of the interest which means whatever amount you are paying as interest will be deducted as tax from the taxable income.

4. You will get the tax benefits if the loan is taken from a bank or any proper financial institution. Loans taken from a friend or a relative will not be considered for tax benefit.

5. Deduction will be up to eight years or till the repayment date; whichever is less can be claimed.

6. You should try to repay the education loan within eight years because if you are still repaying your loan after eight years, you will not get any tax benefits.

7. Deduction will start w.e.f. the date of repayment of loan.

Financial planning

For a secure future, financial planning is a must for every individual. In older age, money security is more important than money liquidity as at that time it is not viable to invest on the risk planning. So it is better to start planning at an earlier age.

Savings and investments should start from the birth of the child. This planning is made, keeping in mind the expenditure required for all the education needs of the child.

Big milestones like higher education, starting businesses and performing marriages need large amounts of money.

If we do not plan early then, we have to face difficulty in unexpected situations like accident, illness, unemployment, loss in business etc.

Budget

Keep an account of your income and expenditure- how much you can earn from different sources and where you have to spend, etc.

Keep 80% of your income for expenditure and rest 20% aside for saving. Also, see where you can reduce expenditure.

With little effort, by lessening expenditures, you can make a suitable budget.

Try to increase your income sources. Try to generate income from your hobby/passion. Teach this habit to your children too.

Don't put extra load on your budget by accepting all the demands of your child.

Keep some money as liquidity with you so that you don't have to ask favours from someone else during times of emergency.

Prevent yourself from taking extra loans.
Try to make the child independent as early as possible.

Savings and investments

Put your money in fixed deposits in banks so that your money is safe and it can be used in times of emergency.

You can get a fixed profit on your investment. For that, different government bonds and post office schemes are there.

If you want a substantial amount after a long time, then you can invest in land, long term shares and mutual funds.

You can also invest in jewellery.

Parents can open their PPF account. It will fulfill your requirements from time to time and will be a regular income source at older age. This is the best and most secure option. Its income is also tax-free.

Property

To arrange for a home in a safe neighbourhood, which may be small but equipped with all facilities, should also be an important part of the financial planning. You can get move out of living in rented houses and leave a house for your children after your death. It will make their life secure.

Nowadays you can purchase a home by taking home loans which is available on low interest and easy instalments. One part of your house can be put on rent and it becomes a regular income.

Insurance

Parents often worry that if some mishap happens and they are not there, who will take care of the children after them. With the help of money their future can be secured.

Parents' life insurance is the best option for it. 10 to 20 times of your annual income should be the covered by life insurance. First priority should be to adopt a term insurance plan. It provides more coverage with less premium.

Financial planning

Insurance has proved to be the best supporter for higher education and to obtain better facilities. The child plans are also like boons for the bright future of a child.

It is a must to get mediclaim insurance and personal accident insurance to protect against expenses in case of sudden illness or sudden accidents.

Will

Parents are required to prepare their will and decide the heir of their money, land and other assets. If you have a business then, indicate who will look after it later. Who will take the responsibility for your child? These types of things are not verbal. Written documents are very important.

Retirement plan

You have to secure not only your child's future but your own future too. It should not happen that while planning for your children you don't save anything for yourself after retirement. Be alert as early as possible. Even if it is only a little money but save positively for the future. Or get a pension plan. After many years this will support you in old age.

Sexual abuse

If a smiling and active child suddenly becomes sad, does not eat, doesn't want to meet anyone, gets easily afraid, then it may be that someone is abusing him. At this age a child doesn't understand sexual harassment and he may also be afraid to say anything. So recognize her/his silence. What to do

The child will recognize people's good or bad intentions when they touch him, especially when you have informed him about it Still it is the duty of the parents to guide him properly. Tell them that he has the full right over his body and should inform the parents if someone touches them or their private parts in an inappropriate way. Along with the girls, boys should also be made aware about it. But don't repeat this matter again and again.

If you suspect something amiss, you should ask the child with love. Ask him if any people around like servants, driver, watchman, teacher, family member etc. has done any unusual activity with her/ him. Then ensure him that he has not done any mistake. The mistake is done by the said person. Along with this, reassure him that he is not bad but he is good.

Let the child continue to go outside and play as before and help him lead a normal life as much as possible.

The gravity of child abuse

- 53.22% children have faced one or more forms of sexual abuse.

- 21.9% children have faced severe forms of sexual abuse and 50.76% other forms of sexual abuse.

Sexual abuse

- 50% children are abused by people known to them.
- 56.37% children are abused in correctional institutions.

Survey report

- 3 in 100 were sexual assaulted (penetration or oral sex); overall, 29% were abused by friends, classmates.
- 12 in 100 were forced to touch private parts; overall 39% by friends classmates.
- 9 in 100 were forced to exhibit private parts; overall 44% by friends classmates.
- 3 out of 100 were photographed in the nude.
- 19 in 100 were forcibly kissed; overall. 35% by friends, classmates. Source: Study on child abuse: India 2007 (conducted on 12,447 children across 13 states).

Avoid misuse of amenities

Get amenities for the children but take care that they may not be inconvenient for children as well as for you.

These days especially, parents get their child equipped with technical amenities, but the child starts misusing them. It is the popular trend nowadays that your child should have a car, motor bike, i-Pod, mobile phone, internet facility etc. But parents should ensure the right use of these by their children and they should not to be absorbed in them all the time.

Many parents are in the rat race to provide all the possible amenities to their child beyond their capacity. Parents, grandparents, aunts, uncles etc. make promises from time to time, to gift things like bike, computer, mobile, etc. for the child if he gets good marks in exams.

To provide amenities to the child is not bad but parents should take care that the child should not misuse them.

Parents should decide which amenity should be given to the child and which should not be.

Get only those things which are helpful in the child's studies. Things must be given for necessity, not for pomp and show.

Sleeping disorder in children

The secret of good health is having sound sleep. Sleep plays a vital role in keeping the body fresh and healthy. Those children who sleep less than needed are often unhealthy and easily irritated. It disturbs their digestive system. They invite diseases like diabetes and heart problems in the future.

Their development stops due to lack of sleep as growth hormone from pituitary glands gets secreted during sleep. Less sleep means less development.

In the earlier time when there was no T.V., computer and mobile games, children often would go to bed after playing and studying and sleep comfortably and remain healthy. But the use of these gadgets has affected the sleep of the children. Late night watching T.V., internet surfing, use of mobile phones has disturbed their sleep badly.

Nowadays, there are separate rooms for children, so parents are less aware about the sleeping disorder of their child.

Parents should form a routine for sleeping and obey it strictly. Talk with the child before sleeping. Don't let him play in the bed room with T.V., computer and video games.

Effects of television

Has an hypnotic effect on children. It drives them away from their study, games and from many other important learning activities. So the habit of children to watch it must be controlled.

The concentration in study decreases. Overeating takes place when eating is done while watching T.V., which results in different diseases like obesity, diabetes, high cholesterol, high blood pressure etc.

Continuously watching T.V. weakens eye sight.

Lack of physical exercise makes the body drowsy.

Problem of sleeping disorder arises.

Children are expert imitators. They try to do whatever they see in T.V. Many times they learn many abusive words from the T.V., even if they don't know the meaning.

Both parents often go to work nowadays. So they provide the amenities like T.V., computer, video games etc. and think that their responsibility is covered. By watching T.V. programmes unsupervised, children try to copy the violent characters they see on T.V., or video games. Anger and fear are primary emotions which are in a child from the beginning and it increases by looking at the violence on television, unsupervised.

The child who is full of aggression from the beginning might become worse as he grows older. Some of such children grow up to be reckless adults who cannot fit into society and cannot follow laws.

Generally, T.V. programmes suited for children are very less. There are few T.V. channels which show knowledgeable and entertaining programmes.

It is also seen nowadays that the parents put on the T.V. to make their child happy, and eventually it becomes their habit. Even small children often become habituated to watching T.V.

Though nowadays it is not possible to keep the child away from the T.V., yet a little control is must.

Fix the time for watching T.V. or playing games. Don't allow him to watch T.V. for more than one hour. Parents should also fix their own time for watching T.V.

Divert the attention of the child. Get him to walk or play in the park. If his energy is not utilized in the right direction, he may deviate.

Hobbies decide the personality of a child. The development of hobbies is the development of personality. These hobbies should not be deformed otherwise these hobbies become curse for the child.

Craze for mobile phones and internet

The chances of depression are considered to be more than double in children who are internet addicts. A study reveals that due to internet, many adolescents may face mental problems.

There is no doubt that internet is an ocean of knowledge and is important for children. But the problem is that, a lot of content in it is harmful for children. So it is better to keep the computer at such a place from where you can check what the child is doing and on which website.

Check the contents of those sites which are frequently visited by your child. If you think that the matter is not suitable to their age, stop the child there.

Check the history of the sites surfed which tells us which site was visited by the child.

Tell him about the ill effects of long talks on the mobile phone on their health and study. To waste so much time can be harmful to their academic studies. Check the mobile phone of your child if you are suspicious of some activity, if there are any obscene messages (SMS) or most messages are deleted then, something might be wrong.

Get a simple mobile for your child which can be used for talking only. A well equipped mobile can make the child busy in playing games, photography, video making and in surfing the internet and waste time better spent in studies or other productive activities.

Save your child from cyber pornography

Sexual curiosity in a child may increase by looking at pornography on the internet. The parents should allow their children access the internet but must keep vigil on them so that they don't indulge in unsuitable activities.

Today mostly all school children are instructed to do their home work and project with the help of a computer. Children are often happy that they can enjoy all the amusement available on the internet. But the child might come across cyber pornography while searching the net.

If the child is stuck to the mobile phone every time or engaged with internet for a long time, then it is not healthy. If the child insists on sitting in front of the computer or makes excuse to work on the computer late at night, or is mostly busy on his mobile phone and tries to conceal it, or if you enter his room and he seems be shocked, then he may be indulging in cyber pornography or such type of SMS.

If your child is found indulging in cyber pornography, then try to understand him and find out where this problem arises from, whether it is from your own house or outside influence

If your child is indulging in bad company then your strictness will not work. It will be better that parents create a healthy environment in the house, sit with the child and try to know his personality. Provide him the right information about sex through good books.

If you want to protect your child from porn sites then use URL (Universal Resource Language) filter or Parental Control Software like Net Nanny, etc. This restricts your child from visiting or encountering porn sites.

To develop talent in children fully, to make them efficient in all activity, to help them realise their good qualities and their defects, and to make them aware of what is right and wrong, parents have to take care at every step.

Teenagers and harmful addictions

During teenage years, often, children take to drinking alcohol for various reasons like keeping up with peer pressure, etc. Parents are also sometimes responsible for letting such habits form.

Due to high expectation from parents, a child may adopt habits of drug addiction or porn movies to cope with the pressure.

Not giving time to children, ignoring them etc. are often the reasons for which the child feels lonely at home and tries to find solace outside in other places.

Specialists say that parents are responsible for the increasing habit of alcohol abuse in children. When a child sees his parent drinking, then he will also adopt the habit. Most children adopt the drinking habit due to the influence of their home environment during teenage years and while an older age, they get the habit from outside.

A child also may see their parents earn wealth the wrong way and also sees their bad habits. At this age, the child is still very emotionally unstable and his habits may start deteriorating.

Those children who start drinking from adolescence often become heavy drinkers as they grow older. Often it is also seen that, in children of middle class families who come into new wealth, drinking starts as a status symbol.

If parents themselves adopt the bad habit of drinking etc. to fit into high society and they drink and smoke before their children, then it is natural that the child will also adopt the same bad habits.

There is also one category of parents who think that their child should do what he wants to do openly in front of them.

Parents of this kind don't see the harm in offering a taste of alcohol to their child in front of them. The parents feel that whatever the child is doing, is in front of them which is better than the children doing it in hiding. These parents forget that a taste of alcohol may become a habit and the situation may be serious.

If we drink, smoke, chew tobacco, etc. and indulge excessively in questionable activities, then how our children will be untouched by these. We have to change ourselves first.

Harmful effects of addictions

A person addicted to drugs can never be healthy or happy. Addiction is akin to cutting one's own feet.

Pan masala, gutka, tobacco, bidi, cigarette, liquor, opium, charas and smack etc. all fall in the category of intoxicating/addictive products.

They are all more harmful than other substances. They seem enjoyable when taken but destroy our body and health.

Tea, coffee and betel leaf are also to a lesser degree seen as detrimental to the life force. All types of intoxicating products are the worst enemies of health. Smoke let out by smoking also harms nonsmokers.

Substance abuse numbs the nerves of a human being, which leads to feeling of constant drowsiness, the brain becomes inactive, the tongue thickens and cannot distinguish taste, the kidneys get damaged, coughing increases and there is gradual loss of teeth. Even in youth, one already feels old. Speech also gets slowed down.

Substance abuse also leads to different types of diseases. It is the root cause of impotency. Nervous tissues and tissues of the brain become inactive. Gradually, life force is reduced and an addicted person's life span is often shorter.

Recognising symptoms of addiction in a child

1. Frequent absence from school, college or work.
2. Staying up late into the night without any reason.
3. Suddenly abandoning old friends for new.
4. Asking frequently for more money to spend than usual.
5. Getting angry without reason suddenly and remarked unusual behaviour.
6. Excessive tiredness, laziness, restlessness, trembling, sweating and dull face.
7. Swelling under the eyes or dirty, reddish eyes.
8. Very low or no interest in social festivals and little patience.
9. Disturbances and change in sleeping pattern.
10. Reduction in digestive power, weight and constant physical weakness
11. Borrowing money or stealing (domestic items disappearing often).
12. Unnecessarily telling lies.
13. Spots of cigarette burns on the body or clothes.
14. Stiffness in the stomach.

What should the parents do?

1. At first the parents are required to have patience. Don't get impatient over the child but try to mend their mistakes slowly.
2. Assure that the child's health is alright and he eats food properly, sleeps sufficiently and does exercises.

3. Parents and teachers should communicate regularly and, they should together help the child.
4. Medical checkup should be done after regular intervals.
5. Encourage the child to work more, exercise and participate in games.
6. Some time should be spent together to promote unity in the family, especially while taking meals.
7. Be thrifty while giving the pocket money but be very loving.
8. Not only cater to your child's physical needs, but also provide for his mental needs, and reassure him.
9. Seek the children's help in domestic activity.
10. Children even like discipline sometimes as it indicates that the parents are paying attention to them.
11. Discuss their problems (if any) in school with patience and in a sensible manner.
12. Never pressure the child with expectations which are impossible to fulfil.
13. Be completely strict but be just.
14. Give positive reinforcements to the child at every step whether he does well or not.
15. Parents are recommended not to consume liquor in front of their children.
16. Be friendly with children.

For an addicted child

1. When you come to know about the addiction of the child, don't scold or beat him. Try to gauge the depth of the problem.

2. At first, get the information from where the child gets these things, who are his friends on whom you have doubts and check his pocket money.
3. Tell him about the harmful effects of addiction.
4. Get him to a counsellor without worrying what people will say because this is a matter of your child's life and future.
5. Before counselling these types of children, parents need to get counselling for themselves.
6. Don't stick to only one way of changing your child. To solve the problems you need to adopt new ways every time.

Ways of giving up addiction

Strong determination, mental strength and the following yogic activity with improved diet can help in giving up addiction.

Shat karma—Kunjal, Sutraneti, Jalneti, Kapalbhati, Shank Prakshalan.

Yogic exercises—Breathing kriya, padmasana, swastikasana, gomukhasana, ardhamatsyendrasana, naukasana, ashwatthanasana, pad-hastasana, naukasana, katichakrasana, garudasana, tadasana, janu shirshasana, paschimottanasana, bhunmanasana, yogmudrasana, shalabhasana, urdhvasarvangasana, halasana, surya namaskar, shavasana.

Pranayama—Nari Shodhan, sheetali, seetkari.

Mahamudra—Ujjai and vipareet karni.

Dhyan—Daily in the morning and evening, practice dhyana and yoga nidra.

Food—Fruits, salad, sprouted grains be taken in increased quantity. 100-200 grams of spinach, cabbage, bathua, coriander, mint leaves, clean radish leaves, turnip leaves and other eatable leaves daily to be washed and eaten for helping in getting rid of intoxication.

Special—Those who wish to give up smoking, gutka, tobacco etc. should take a piece of small harad in their mouth and suck its juice whenever the desire to take the substance arises. After a few days or longer, they will get over this habit.

Prevent criminal tendencies in the child

Criminal tendencies are increasing in children. Due to the rise and spread of luxuries and changing values, their desires are increasing and when it doesn't get fulfilled, they are seen to many times, adopt the way of crime.

Children often find thieving or snatching things the easiest way to fulfil their wants.

Selling sex, theft, plunder, kidnapping, murder and all other types of crime have become common even in children.

Violence is starting to dominate the child. Changing social environment, changing priorities and changing attitudes are making children increasingly aggressive.

Teenagers are often accused for the increasing violent behaviours but the truth is that, our own people and community is more responsible for their violent behaviour. The reality is that many things that a child get from his parents is filled with violence like toys to video games, films, serials, internet, cartoon channels and comics etc. Family and social environment, too many amenities, parents' lack of free time, bad company of other children may be the causes of their violent behaviour.

Specialists think that these things, given above, make the child violent, because eventually we become what we listen to, see, read, and eat.

How can we recognise such behaviour

If a child gets angry unreasonably, howls and cries on trifle things, hurts himself or others in anger, breaks things in anger, teases younger children aggressively, fights on any given occasion then, it is sure that his behaviour is violent.

What to do when you recognize this

If violent behaviour is observed in teenagers then, consult a specialist immediately.

The sooner you find a remedy, the easier it will be to solve the problem. The main aim of the remedy is to tell the child how he can control his anger and how he can cool down in a proper place. Counselling can also be done after understanding his personal, family and social problems and attitude. This needs co-operation from his family, friends, teacher and community.

Prevention

Prevention is always better than cure so, care should be taken from the beginning so that they don't get attracted towards crime.

Mother and Father

The first contact of a child with the world is his parents. It is believed that the criminal tendency of a child may start from the pregnancy period itself if the parents live unethically. The life style and attitude of mother during pregnancy affects the child. For example, if a lady constantly faces excitement and anger during pregnancy then her child may also become excited and angry. There is no doubt that behind the criminal tendency of many children, the nature of the parents can be held responsible.

After birth, most of the child's life depends on the parents' behaviour. Many times, they become culprits due to the strict and rude behaviour of their parents, teacher or guardians. In this condition they are pleased by lashing out at others. They feel proud of disobeying their elders and rebelling against them. It becomes their habit in the future. They may also enjoy abusing their siblings.

When you are too strict with children or criticise them too much, then they become more persistent towards doing things you dislike. Even rude words, harmless as they sound, gradually affect the child.

Don't doubt the child and don't conceal anything from him.

If your behaviour with the child is improved, then he can be saved from criminal activities to a great degree.

Don't hold back in appreciating their good work.

Diet

If virtuous food (fruits, vegetable, juices, etc.) is given to the child from beginning, then the child gets the best accomplishments.

Toys

Nobody realises that when he puts a toy pistol in the hands of a child, that it will affect his mind adversely and on the basis of this, his thoughts develops.

If a child likes to play with violent toys always, then stop him there. For example, if any child plays with the toys of rifle/pistol too much then, this is a warning for the parents.

Discrimination

Excess love for one and less to other should not be in any house. Children want justified behaviour from you. If you are not behaving same for both of them then, they might quarrel too often and might turn to the direction of criminal activities.

Deformed attitude of the society

Due to narrow attitude of our society, if a child makes a mistake then he is treated as faulty. We show bad attitude towards him and he is humiliated occasionally. Due to this, many children turn violent. To make a mistake is human nature. If you don't punish excessively the basic mistake of children, and have good behaviour with them then, they can be improved.

Emotional attachment

A child may be given everything which can be purchased by money but the parents may have no time for their children. A child has to face many problems and they want to share it with their parents. When they don't get co-operation from the parents, they take the help of their friends.

The friends guide him according to their thinking. As a result of this, sometimes they may turn to a wrong way.

Those parents who are busy in their careers and don't have an interest in their child's life, their children often generally go on the wrong path. A child has the nature of being impulsive, and when he does not get right direction he turns to the wrong path. Those people who do not have time for their children like maybe politicians or social workers, their children may go on the wrong track.

If you are not able to give time to your children due to your busy schedule then, you can take them on weekend holidays, so that your child can share everything of the whole week with you and doesn't feel lonely. So try to give maximum time to your child whenever you can. Take him on walks in the evening and morning.

The effect of T.V., internet and films

Studies reveal that children often learn the attitude and ways of crime from T.V. serials, films, internet and video games. It is the advice of specialists that children should be banned from violent programmes and the use of internet should be under the observation of elders. CD players should not be kept in children's room as many types of CDs are available freely in the market which may influence the child to be violent.

Family atmosphere

Mutual disputes and misbehaviour of the parents affects the children adversely. The quarrelsome life and bad character of the parents are also the reason for making the child violent.

Parents should think about how their own quarrels can affect the children.

Be careful that family members are nor aggressive towards with one another. Don't shout and scream when you talk with each other as children learn a lot from you.

Bad company

Even a good child becomes bad when he falls into bad company. The receptive but indiscriminating mind gets attracted easily towards evil. The root cause of the evil in a child rises from the bad company. If no attention is paid, child may get in to bad company.

Scolding

Research tells that those children who are scolded or beaten at home get inferiority complex. They think themselves to be weak and helpless. As they cannot rebel outwardly, their anger becomes concentrated inside them. Don't scold or beat your child. Correct their mistake with love and affection.

Avoid the child from misusing his anger

If the parents fulfil all the demands of a child when he is angry, then he thinks of himself as the winner. He then starts using his anger for getting his improper demands too. So do not fulfil all his demands out of fear for the child's anger.

Excessive amenities is also a problem

Fulfilling all the demands of the child, boasting before him of your richness and making him feel that he is the child of a rich person is the root cause for the child to be spoiled. Even if the parents are wealthy, they should not tell to their child. If you tell them then, also tell them that how much you have to work to earn that money. Then they will know the importance of everything.

Keep away deadly weapons out of the reach of children

If you have revolvers or sharp weapons in your house for security purposes then, keep them out of reach of the children.

Never talk about these things before the child

Tell them the rules are made for the benefit of society. Violation of rules results in punishment. Parents should also tell their children that being wealthy and powerful does not mean breaking the rules. Rules are same for everyone irrespective of wealth and power.

Responsibilities of teaching institutions

In many teaching institutions, due to the questionable character of teachers, the children may get bad habits. It is easy to imagine what can be learnt by students from those teachers who smoke before the children, gambles and gossip with their friends and talk using vulgar language. There is no doubt that students copy their teacher and try to do what the teacher does.

Adolescence/Teenage years

There is a time of great tussle between parents and children during the teenage years. Parents think that the children do not hear them and children think that parents interfere in every matter. During this phase, a child gets his information from friends, media, T.V., films and internet etc. At this age, 'I' and 'my choice' becomes the prime thing for a child.

This is ideally the age for studying well, eating well, physical and mental development. During this age the bones muscles and sex organs develop specifically. With the body, habits and nature also change. During this period they get increasingly attracted towards the opposite sex. Facial hair appears in a boy and growth of breasts appears in the girl during this age. They start taking interest in sex. Sex organs develop and enlarge which is natural. This is the time when children are growing into adulthood. This is the period when the child enters into youth. During this age, children are often busy in their studies and they also remain in the atmosphere of games, sports, enjoyment etc.

Girls should get nutritious meals during menstrual periods. During this period, secretion of blood occurs and the body becomes weak. During this, the girl may have complaints of back pain, excess secretion of blood or discomfort due to it. They may be easily irritated and could lose interest in doing work etc. During this period, an iron and calcium-rich diet like plenty of green vegetables, fresh fruit juice, milk, butter, cheese, curd, lassi and dry fruits is the best meal for them.

During this age, a child wants to live free. Due to this they express their views openly and a child fulfils his desire occasionally by arguing with his parents.

Many times he opposes his parents on many matters

The increasing attraction towards the opposite sex is a common thing during this age. To keep them within acceptable limits, parents have to exercise control and discipline.

Don't put such restrictions on them which compel them to rebel and later make it their habit.

But ban is must for drugs, alcohol, smoking etc.

Friendly behaviour

When a child enters into his teenage years, parents should behave with him like a friend.

Rash driving

Many children are addicted for high speed driving. Don't give a bike or car to a child below 18 years. Tell them that this may put him behind bars or someone may lose his life.

Dating and party

As long as the child tells you about where he is going, with whom he is going, when he will come back, then nothing is wrong. But even if he is concealing something from you then, don't scold him, at least not in front of somebody else. Tell him the responsibilities that come along with freedom, if possible send him in a group. Ask him before leaving about where he is going and when he will come back. Don't allow late night parties. Send them on school tours but abstain from sending them with friends for other outdoor tours.

Knowledge of safe sex

Sex is a part of life. If a child gets proper information, he will hold the right view. If he asks any question, then don't reprimand him. You should be proud that your child has trust on you. Tell him about the reproduction of plants, animals and then, of human beings. Try to support your child in such a way that he indulge in sex before the right time.

Freedom

Children want freedom today. They don't like interruptions, limitations from the parents. They may be rebellious if the parents put their own wishes on them.

Don't make him go over his mistake repeatedly. Don't compel him for to do anything. It will be better that you give two options and tell him the results of both options. He will choose the right option.

Parents are always in a dilemma about the freedom of their children. They want to give freedom to their children as per the requirements of today but due to being anxious about their safety, they also want to impose restrictions.

Specify the time limit to children up to which they can stay out, so that they have the knowledge as to how much freedom the parents want to give them.

Generation gap

The difference in views between two generations has been seen since time immemorial. The reason is that, elders do not want the younger ones to retort back at them. And younger ones cannot bear the monopoly of elders over opinions. The result is that there is a tussle.

Tradition, rule and regulations keep changing with time. So change takes place in the society.

The old generation may not be ready to accept that change which has become compulsory for the new generation.

An old person cannot bear opposition from the youngsters as they consider that youngsters should obey him blindly. Whatever the older says is correct and left over is considered rubbish and destructive. A youngster arguing back is not liked by the old generation. It is not necessary that younger ones accept everything blindly. Due to fear of beating, often children accept the verdict when they are young but their heart doesn't accept it. This confusion makes them disturbed internally and develops an aggression in them, which after a stage becomes explosive.

Now the demand of the times is that we have to think ourselves as a friend to our offspring by leaving the thinking that we are elder and thus need to be obeyed blindly. Utilize more time with your children and recognize their needs.

So deal with the child tenderly and make them understand what is right and what is wrong.

Talk is a must between the parents and children. Talks should be from both sides. Parents should be a good listener and listen carefully to the child too. It should not be that you order something and the child has to follow that.

Include him in decision making. Take his consent while making the home menu, rules for study, play, etc. Also decide together on the punishment for breaking a rule. Decide holiday schedules with him as to how long he will study and how long he will watch T.V.

Be a part of the world of the child. Talk to him at his level. The talk should not be childish but should be in a matured way.

> **A child gets developed by his imagination. We should not stop his imagination. We should also save them from getting damaged.**

Abnormal children and their special care

The child which has lesser IQ than considered normal or there is a physical deformity in his body or those who is mentally under developed is called an abnormal or differently-abled child.

Mentally deficient children

1. The intelligence quotient (IQ) in such children is generally less than 70
2. Understanding is slow in such children.
3. They are much more suggestible.
4. They have less self confidence and self dependency.
5. They have less adjustment ability.
6. They have no ability to learn or to take benefit from past experience.
7. They have limited hobbies.
8. They have the feelings of fear and insecurity.
9. They lack interest in intimacy.
10. They are much creative than others.
11. They are slow learners but sometimes their IQ score may be more than the normal ones.

Dyslexia

This is a learning disorder. The child who suffers from this disorder has a problem in reading and writing. The main problem is that he cannot recognize the letters (of alphabet) properly. They can understand everything by hearing but they have some confusion in reading. The child remains confused mainly for those words which are alike in appearance or in sound. For example,'d' and 'b', or, '7' and 'L'. Sometimes the child makes mistake in spellings. Mirror image is written correctly, for example 'was' is written as 'saw'.

This is a neurological problem and many a times it is genetic. It is not related to intelligence. This problem may happen with any child of low IQ, normal IQ or high IQ. Mostly the parents and teachers think that the child is disobedient but the reason behind it is the learning disorder.

This disorder is recognizable if the child has a lower IQ than his peers in class or other children of the same age group, and mostly repeats the same type of mistakes.

Reason for abnormality

During pregnancy, the mother's consumption of alcohol, smoking, drugs or taking medicine for mental diseases, increases the chances of mental or physical deformity in the child.

The nervous system of a child gets destroyed by high blood pressure or blood poisoning infection of a pregnant mother.

A severe disease in childhood may cause infection which also destroys the cells of brain. Falling down and hitting the head during childhood or shaking the head severely by any elder may cause this problem. The child may also become abnormal due to poverty, malnutrition, lack of hygiene (filth) and not getting proper treatment at right time.

Instructions for the parents

If your child is differently-abled then, instead of cursing yourself or your child, accept it as a challenge.

Always remember that you are not the only parents who are facing such problems. Many parents in this world are nourishing such children.

The child is yours and so the related problems will be yours. You have given birth to him so you have to accept all his abilities or disabilities.

Parents should be fully devoted in nourishing an abnormal child but other family members should also co-operate them. Relatives should behave with him appropriately, understanding his sensitivity. Don't show your pity by considering him helpless.

Parents should behave with the child in such a manner that his feeling of fear, insecurity and hesitation gradually starts reducing. The child should not feel afraid and hesitated.

The family, social, educational and occupational needs of such children are more than the other children. So fulfil them.

Highly abnormal children often trouble their parents. So maintain your patience and mental balance.

Special care of an abnormal child

Adequate care and love from parents can help teach them how to live a normal life. Don't discourage them when they are not that good in academics. Recognize their other abilities and encourage them to do well in that field.

The irony is that most parents force them to study and by comparing them with other children they decrease the self confidence of such children.

Admire the work in which the child has ability. It will bring self confidence in him and feelings of hesitation will be removed.

Parents and teachers should not scold the child. Pay more attention to him and advice him gently. Recognize his creativity and encourage him to manifest them. If necessary take the help of a psychiatrist.

Make them understand by giving simple examples. Take help of special audio-visuals aid to teach them.

The main thing is that parents and relatives should understand his problems and enhance his talent in the fields where he can do better.

His interests may be in singing, playing, dancing, acting, technical works, etc. where he can perform better. The need is to encourage them and help them opt for such an education where their talents will shine. Sometimes parents lack time to pay attention due to which the child becomes stubborn and bad natured. So parents must pay adequate time especially to such children. Instead of simply giving sympathy, compel such children to be more independent but in a disciplined way.

You will not always be there to help him. So as much as possible make him independent to live in the society. Let him do his own daily work like bathing, washing, eating, etc.

Education

The curriculum for differently-abled children should be different from that of a normal student.

Special Class — Due to many reasons, experts have advised to educate mentally deficient children in special classes. Such classes are beneficial for the student as it becomes possible for the teacher to pay maximum attention on each individual student. The student doesn't feel an inferiority complex as there are no advanced students as in a normal class who would make fun of his thoughts.

Teaching Method — To provide education to such a child, demonstration method is the best. Insist on the method of self learning by doing works or working on crafts himself.

Teachers should tell them to do their work themselves according to their basic requirements. Then provide them vocational training according to their ability and let them live their life self dependent in the society.

There are many examples where abnormal children have surprised the world by doing marvellous works. Such children may have talents like famous scientist Albert Einstein and Newton, artists Pablo Piccaso and Leonardo Da Vinci, famous cartoonist Walt Disney or Bollywood star Abhishek Bachchan. The need is to recognise and to enhance his talent. The expert says that these famous personalities in childhood suffered from dyslexia or attention deficient hyperactivity disorder type learning problems. Still, they achieved such high goals in their life.

Helen Keller was the first human being who after being deaf, dumb and blind got a graduate degree. Her saying was that life is not meant to run from the problems but it is to win over the problems.

Special planning for differently-abled children

1. When such a child grows up, it is not always possible that such children can earn for themselves in life. So parents have to ensure that he doesn't have to depend on others in life. Arrange adequate funds for him. Even if the child is able to earn something himself still you should plan for him so that he has adequate money from alternative sources.

2. Parents of such children should ensure a permanent residence for such children.

3. Parents should purchase a good maturity value insurance policy which can fulfil the requirements of such children after their deaths.

4. Ensure that the amount you are saving for your child reaches his hands safely. You can do it through a trust which will dispense the money according to when and how much amount should be given to your child. For the need of children you can form a trust. It will be better to make the trust in your presence and take legal advice for

it. It should be mentioned in the trust deed, what you want and what decision should be taken at what time. Regulations of the trust must be defined according to the requirements of the child. It will be better to appoint more than one trustee and their ages should be less than yours.

5. For such a child, be sure to make a will and mention all details of assets and liquid fund. Financial experts' advice is to appoint a person to implement their will, so that their child gets all the wealth in the right way.

6. The person(s) who has been appointed by the parents may become guardian of such children after the death of parents.

Childlessness

Not getting a child after a long trial, can become the reason for depression.

For the birth of a child, a man contributes sperm and a woman contributes the egg. Problem of infertility may be either physical or mental.

Age, obesity, malnutrition, tension, smoking or alcohol addiction may cause this problem. Physical or untreated chronic diseases also becomes the cause of childlessness.

After a late marriage, preventing pregnancy for the sake of career can also become the cause of childlessness.

Solution

1. Those physical and mental problem whose treatment is possible, be treated. Take the help of naturopathy also.
2. For those women who have the fallopian tube blocked or damaged or whose ovary is normal but menstrual period does not occur then Invitro Fertilization Technique (IVF) is used for conceiving. In this technique, with the help of sonography, the egg is taken out to get it fertilized in a laboratory and then put into the uterus. Due to this technique a lot of women's dream of becoming a mother has come true.
3. Those women who cannot conceive due to obstruction in uterus can get the obstruction removed with the help of hysteroscopy technique.
4. Many times due to defect of the ovary, eggs formation does not take place in women. In this condition, they can be a mother if any other woman donates her eggs and they be fertilized by the sperm of the husband of that

women and then put in her uterus. With the help of this technique, women can become a mother after menopause also.

5. If sperms are not coming out due to blockage in urinal tube then they can be taken out with the help of a fine needle from the scrotum/testis and can produce a baby by test tube technique.

6. Today surrogacy is has become popular. Due to problem in conceiving, those people who cannot become parents, they take the help of other women. This is surrogacy. The egg and sperm of the parents is fertilized outside and put in the uterus of a surrogate mother. In this technique, egg and sperm both are of real parents and the foetus is nourished in some other woman's uterus. When the child takes birth then it is given to the biological mother and father legally. This hired mother doesn't have physical relation to the child. If the child is tested for DNA, then nothing will appear of surrogate mother. If the husband is physically fit and wife's ovulation is normal, but foetus is not developing in uterus or uterus is not fit to hold the foetus for nine months or there is cancer in the ovary or heart problems in woman or retina detention in eyes and which may lead to eye loss on conceiving then, in all these situations, surrogacy is preferred.

If after all medication and trials you are still not able to get a child then it is better that you adopt an orphan child and make yours and his life fruitful.

> **Children woman should behave with other's children in a motherhood way, this increases the possibility of their being mother due to hormonal change.**

Divorce and the children

Divorce affects children badly. It doesn't matter at what age they are. Family division is not good for children.

The reality is that after getting a stamp of divorce, the life does not remain normal.

Both wife and husband have troubles as divorce is a painful act. So try your best so that situation may not arise for a divorce. Think about saving the marriage, not to ruin it.

Think about your children. When you get divorced due to your own ego then what will happen to your children? The children of divorced parents usually become rebellious or irritating or sometimes insecure.

After the marriage it is better to forget your ego. Remember the tree which has more fruits is bowed down. It is better for one to remain quiet if the other is in anger. Otherwise the fight will increase.

In brief, we can say that if the situation of divorce comes when the mother or father try to get rid of a situation. Marriage is a beautiful relation. Try to keep its fragrance forever. Quarrels and fights are momentary. Don't let the situation go on till divorce is inevitable.

Remember that children want to see the parents together.

When any one (wife-husband) tries to mend the relation between them, no one gets defeated. But it makes the relation more affectionate.

Company of grandparents gives satisfaction to children

Encourage your children to live with grandparents. Grandparents are better teachers than parents in many aspects, because they have lot more of experience of their past.

Research has found that children want to share their school and college experience in the home, but at the stage of dissociation they accept their grandparents as their friends. They talk about everything with them and get satisfied.

Children of single parents or step parents feel secure and happy with their grandparents.

Grandparents play an important role in divorced families. When the child gets the company of their grandparents, they forget the separation of their parents and their mental development is unaffected. Those children who remain with step parents feel secure with their grandparents. They have the courage to express their views with them.

Children's job/occupation

Not getting a job after the completion of graduation can distress anyone. At that time you can help them to continue their study or in selection for their career. This way they will get help to fight with the forthcoming problems in their life. Most of the young people think that without a job their life is meaningless. It is obvious that they need support from their family during this time. You should help them to be a part of the society, so that they can get self confidence.

Whatever business you are doing, you should not compel your child to adopt that. Don't tie your child with you unwillingly.

Many parents put responsibilities on children much later but then it is too late.

If you have provided a new business for him then, look after it from time to time.

When we set a goal with our burning desire, then our sub conscious mind starts working fast and search for new ways itself. And it is sure to get success.

Marriage of children

Marriage is considered an unbreakable attachment for a couple. Marriage is one of the important decisions of the life. So take decision regarding it with patience, caution and after investigation.

Till the boy gets a good job and accepts his responsibility, don't get him married. Teach all house hold activities to the girl before marriage.

Don't get children married when they are underage. It will be harmful for them and for their children. The minimum legal age of girl is 18 years and that of boy is 21 years.

Age difference between wife and husband

Difference of 5-9 years of age between husband and wife is normal but in no case the age of wife should be greater than husband. In same age or more age women get menopause before the sexual satisfaction of the husband.

So for the harmonious co-ordination in sexual satisfaction of both man and women, age difference is the main factor.

Thalassaemia Minor/Trait Test

(By a special test HbQ2) if a person has thalassaemia minor trait then, he or she should not get married with people having the same problem. Thalassaemia minor trait is not manifested in the host. They live a normal life as others.

But if both have thalassaemia minor trait, then the possibility is that the child will be thalassaemia major (patient).

Pre marriage counselling

The main aim of pre marriage counselling is to provide complete information to the young generation about marriage and married life, so that both the young man and woman can give respect to each other and live a loving and encompassing life.

For a happy married life, knowledge and healthy sexual relationship is necessary.

A balanced family relation gives a happy married life.

Before choosing groom

Inquire about his self dependency, responsibilities, qualification, talent, character and behaviour. Get all the information about his gentle and balanced way of talking, his sense of humour, his intelligence etc. In order to choose a supreme and suitable groom for your daughter, try your best as per your capacity but respect her emotions too.

Before choosing bride

1. As much as possible, get a bride from a family of your level.
2. Give preference to the education, culture and qualities of the girl instead of her beauty.
3. Inform the girl about your family background clearly and correctly.
4. Check it earlier that the expenditure of the girl is not too high so that your income will be sufficient.
5. Choose a bride who understands the expectations of you and your family and respects the sentiments of all.
6. As long as possible choose a soft spoken, polite and compatible bride.
7. Know about the desires and expectations of the girl by meeting her. If you cannot fulfil her expectation then, choose another girl.

8. Think well before choosing a beautiful, well educated and modern bride as to whether she will get adjusted in your family or not. Generally in traditional families, the bride of modern views cannot adjust and a tussle is always seen.

When the boy who prefers beauty only, he faces difficulties after marriage. He doesn't need a beautiful wife but needs a good companion who can understand his sentiments and respect him. But a girl with an ego about her beauty and who is far from traditions cannot be a good companion. But if we talk about behaviour then, a girl's good quality and culture are her real recognition. A girl with the assets of good qualities, behaviour and culture will make that house heaven in which she gets married.

> **A marriage which stands on greed and false expectations, is most controversial than any other thing for a family.**

Daughter-in-law of a family

The daughter-in-law of a family is the base for the coming generation of your family. So just as the son is treated the daughter-in-law should also be treated in the same way. She should be given respect. She should be given recognition. Her opinion should have an importance in the family.

A wife will never want that his husband should not care for his own mother but she would also want that he should not be so dedicated to his mother that he doesn't care for her.

The life becomes easy if the mother-in-law doesn't think that the daughter in law will drive her son away from her. Whenever she offers a good shirt to your son, don't stare at her. She is not doing that to drive your son away from you. If you let it be then, gradually she can be your best friend.

The care which a daughter-in-law gets in a family is generally less than what she deserves. Don't taunt or misbehave with her even by mistake.

The children, no matter how little they may be, when they see their mother is always troubled due to taunts, it can affect their mind adversely. So, not for anyone else but for your own grandchildren's sake, stop taunting your daughter-in-law.

In a new family, a little affection from mother-in-law fills the daughter-in-law with pleasure.

Inducing letter

(A letter written by a famous businessman Sh. Ghanshyam Dass Birla ji to his son Shri Basant Kumar Birla)

Live long Basant,
This is what I am writing, read it when you grow matured and even when you grow old. I am saying this of my own experience. To get a human life is difficult. This is true that after getting a human life that he who has misused is like an animal. You have money and health and good means and if you use them for devotion then these means are good otherwise they are the tools of a devil. You keep it in mind always.

Don't use money for luxuries. Money will not remain always but till it is with you, use it for devotion. Spend a little for yourself. Use the balance for eradicating miseries of poor.

Money is power and it's ego can do injustice with someone. Remember this thing always. Leave this message for your children too. If the children are luxurious, they will commit a sin.

Don't forget the old parents

Those who ignore their seniors should not forget that they have to face it themselves someday.

The sacrifice and duty which you have done or you are doing for your children, your parents must have done that for you.

If you ignore your aged parents then, your children will also ignore you one day.

Older people have a good and long experience of the life. If today's generation takes advantage from their experiences then, they may get solutions of many problems.

Those who give service and respect to their parents and seniors always get blessing and success in life.

> **This is foolishness if you feel ashamed of your elders for not being modern.**

Holistic Health and Wellness from STERLING

This series of guides lets you into the secrets of better health care and also gives you an insight into the causes of diseases and the ways to cure them.

Fit for Life through Ayurveda
Vaidya Suresh Chaturvedi
978 81 207 3975 8
₹ 75

The Secret Benefits of Aroma Therapy
Sumeet Sharma
978 81 207 3996 3
₹ 75

The Secret Benefits of Aloevera
Vijaya Kumar
978 81 207 5606 9
₹ 75

The Secret Benefits of Lemon and Honey
Vijaya Kumar
978 81 207 5577 2
₹ 75

The Secret Benefits of Onion and Garlic
Vijaya Kumar
978 81 207 5578 9
₹ 75

The Secret Benefits of Juice Therapy
Vijaya Kumar
978 81 207 6577 1
₹ 75

The Secret Benefits of Spices and Condiments
Vijaya Kumar
978 81 207 5576 5
₹ 75

The Secret Benefits of Ginger and Turmeric
Vikaas Budhwaar
978 81 207 6576 4
₹ 75

The Secret Benefits of Yoga and Naturopathy for Women
Parvesh Handa
978 81 207 3514 9
₹ 100

Secret Tips to Ultimate
Beauty
Vijaya Kumar
978 81 207 7039 3
₹ 75

The Scientific Way to
Managing Obesity
Dr. Mini Sheth & Nirali Shah
978 81 207 3189 9
₹ 150

How to Control Asthma
and Allergy
Rajeev Sharma
1 84557 534 2
₹ 75

The Healing Powers of Herbs
Ranjit Roy Chaudhury
978 81 207 3319 0
₹ 125

The Benefits of Vitamins
Pooja Bajaj Malhotra
978 81 207 6575 7
₹ 75

The Benefits of
Homoeopathy
Vijaya Kumar
978 18557 626 4
₹ 75

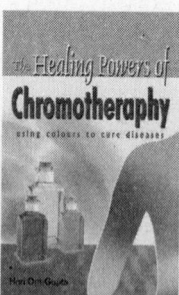

The Healing Powers of
Chromotheraphy
Hari Om Gupta
978 81 207 3253 7
₹ 125

How to Control Wrinkles
and Ageing
Parvesh Handa
978 81 207 5586 4
₹ 99

Beauty and Health
through Ayurveda
Vaidya Suresh Chaturvedi
978 81 207 3268 1
₹ 75

Speaking of Curing Diseases
through Yoga
Swami Durganand Saraswati
978 81 207 6377 7
₹ 175

Yoga and Nature-Cure
Therapy
K S Joshi
978 184557 045 3
₹ 85

Nature Cure
K Lakshmana Sarma &
S Swaminathan
978 81 207 7314 1
₹ 85

Stress Management
through Yoga and
Meditation
Pt. Shambhu Nath
1 84557 311 9
₹ 75

Nutrition & Health: The
Vegetarian Way
INYS
978 81 207 6902 1
₹ 150

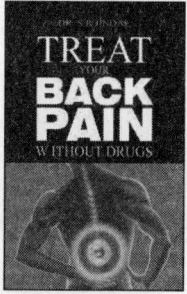

Treat Your Back Pain
without Drugs
Dr S R Jindal
978 81 207 2450 1
₹ 75

Nature Cure: Healing
without Drugs
INYS
978 81 207 2447 1
₹ 90

Eating for a Healthy Life
Deepa Mehta
978 81 207 1983 5
₹ 90

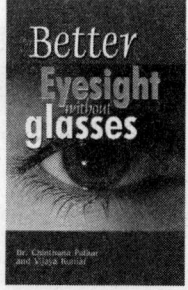

Better Eyesight without
Glasses
Dr. Chinthana Patkar and
Vijaya Kumar
978 81 207 5892 6
₹ 75

Books by Dr. Brij Bhushan Goel

For catalogue write to:

Sterling Publishers (P) Ltd.
A-59, Okhla Industrial Area,
Phase-II, New Delhi-110020.
Tel: 26387070, 26386209;
Fax: 91-11-26383788
E-mail: mail@sterlingpublishers.com
www.sterlingpublishers.com